THE Sound OF Story

Developing **Voice and Tone** in Writing

This morning my hands are so hot, sweat slides my mug out of my grasp and coffee spills down my right leg, like liquid fire. On the way to the bus in the pre-sunrise dark, a voice the past drifts to radio t

JORDAN ROSENFELD

Sibylline
PRESS

AN IMPRINT OF ALL THINGS BOOK

Sibylline Press

Copyright © 2026 by Jordan Rosenfeld
All Rights Reserved.

Published in the United States by Sibylline Press, an imprint of All Things Book LLC, California.

Sibylline Press is dedicated to publishing the brilliant work of women authors ages 50 and older.
www.sibyllinepress.com

Print ISBN: 9798897400041
Ebook ISBN: 9798897400058
Library of Congress Control Number: 2025934045

Book and Cover Design & Production: Alicia Feltman

HUMAN AUTHORED: Any use of this publication to train generative artificial intelligence (AI) technologies to generate text is expressly prohibited.

PRAISE FOR JORDAN ROSENFELD'S

The Sound of Story

"Warning: *The Sound of Story* by Jordan Rosenfeld is the only book on writing an authentic story you will ever need."

—Linda Joy Myers, founder National Association of Memoir Writers, author of *Don't Call Me Mother*

* * *

"Rosenfeld offers a fresh and accessible look at voice ... for deepening characterization in the service of complex and multi-layered storytelling."

—Sonya Huber, *Voice First: A Writer's Manifesto*

* * *

"Peppered with insights, examples, and creative exercises ... this voice-centered resource is a must-read for writers at any stage of their careers."

—Laura Stanfill, author of *Imagine a Door*

* * *

"Few writing teachers understand the subtleties of voice and tone as deeply or can explain them as clearly as Jordan Rosenfeld ... A great resource for fiction and nonfiction writers alike."

—Martha Alderson, author of *The Plot Whisperer* and *Parallel Lives: A 60's Love Story*.

"Rosenfeld takes the ineffable quality of voice, the very quality that sells novels and stories and is demanded by agents and editors, and breaks it down into practical tools and approaches that can help any writer at any stage in their work dig a little deeper and make their prose sing."

—Kate Maruyama author of *Alterations, The Collective,* and *Bleak Houses*

* * *

"A craft book with its own compelling voice, Jordan Rosenfeld's *The Sound of Story* opens the toolbox for 'the sound ... the energy, motion and rhythm ... the emotion' of voice. Rich sample passages suggest a wealth of strategies and her brilliant prompts offer ways to create a narrative voice true to character and story. Your writing will be changed, no question."

–Beverly Burch, author of *What You Don't Know*

Dedicated, in memory, to Bob Finertie,

who fought his way back to his voice and inspired many along the way.

Table of Contents

PART ONE: Complexities of Voice 1

   i. Introduction 3

   1. Voice as Backstory and History 13
   2. Voice as Specificity 37
   3. Voice as Emotional Expression 55
   4. Voice as Opinion and Judgment 87
   5. Narrative Voice vs. Character Voice in Fiction 109
   6. Voice in Memoir and Essay 129

PART TWO: Mechanisms of Voice 149

   7. Syntax and Lexicon 151
   8. Jargon, Slang, and Code-Switching 179
   9. How Genre Shapes Voice 197
   10. Making Sentences Sing: Rhythm and Musicality 213
   11. Cutting Sentence Clutter 243

PART THREE: Shaping Tone 261

   12. Tone Evokes a Feeling 263
   13. Tone in Thoughts and Dialogue 283
   14. Creating Tone Through Imagery 301
   15. Tone in Genre 321

PART FOUR: Final Voice Notes 335

16. Voice in Nonfiction: Objectivity and Personality 337
17. Experimenting with Voice.. 357
18. The Power and Evolution of Voice.. 373

PART ONE

Complexities of Voice

Introduction

> "I wouldn't be surprised if poetry—poetry in the broadest sense, in the sense of a world filled with metaphor, rhyme, and recurring patterns, shapes and designs—is how the world works."
>
> —David Byrne

What is Voice?

"Voice" in writing may be a confusing buzzword: ethereal and innate, yet maddeningly concrete. You may know it when you read it, and agents and publishers often request that a book be rich with it, but what *is* it? Hopefully, the title of this book is a good giveaway, with the *sound of story* tipping you off—though "sound" only scratches the surface. This is the magic of language: It is auditory; it is visual; it is kinetic, as in American Sign Language; and it is tactile—think of the raised dots of Braille with which some blind people may still read. Language that we read with our eyes also has an inner rhythm, which writer Jane

Alison describes as "a felt motionless movement through space" in her book *Meander, Spiral, Explode: Design and Pattern in Narrative*. Thus, voice is also energy, motion, and rhythm.

On the technical end, voice is trussed and undergirded by mechanics that make phrases, sentences, and paragraphs flow in a particular manner through syntax, grammar, and other linguistic techniques. Yet our sentences don't emerge from some vacuum or ether—how and why people and characters express themselves stems from deeper influences. Voice, then, is as much a representation of the who, what, and why of your characters and narrator—their tastes, interests, terrors, desires, and all the complexities that shape their personalities and attitudes. (A note: When referring to the "character" at the center of memoir or essay, I'll be using the term "the narrator" to suggest someone who is both you and not you, a created avatar for the page that can be helpful to think of as a character one step removed from you.)

Voice is also a glimpse into the world from which your character or narrator has sprung: the region they may hail from; the dictates, rules, and structures imparted by a family, a culture, or the historical period; to name a few influences. Voice also emerges from the way emotion shapes expression, the way attitudes crest into conversation, the way thoughts dictate action. Just as fingerprints and snowflakes are all unique, so are voices, though they may hold echoes of the "containers" in which they're grown. It is precisely when and how we latch onto that individuality as writers that voice springs alive on the page. Voice is also attitude and opinion, a judgmental rut, an optimistic pronouncement.

Many genres in the canon of United States literature have a relatively unique voice signature or style that readers come to expect, which make it possible to identify the genre within a few pages. While there is more genre bending and leaping than ever these days, sometimes knowing what the voice demands of a genre are can help you increase your chances of publication within that genre.

It's impossible to explore voice without exploring perspective / point of view. Some voices are intimately in the "I," the reader so close to the character / narrator, there's no space to even encounter a self. Others are omniscient, a lording presence that tells all without character permission. This, too, shapes how we perceive and experience voice. The memoirist / essayist may have to play with literary devices like letters and texts to give voice to experiences they are only adjacent to, while laying their own voice as bare as can be.

Though much of voice is also sentence- and grammar-level mechanics, I am neither a linguist, a grammarian, nor an English teacher. So while we will touch on sentences, because it's impossible not to, I highly recommend you turn to other books for that, such as Nina Schuyler's *How* to *Write Stunning Sentences,* Constance Hale's *Sin and Syntax: How to Craft Wickedly Effective Prose,* or Reuven Tsur's *What Makes Sound Patterns Expressive? The Poetic Mode of Speech Perception.*

Additionally, while this book is full of writerly advice and examples, it does not purport to be universal. Regardless of how widely I think I read across genres, cultures, and more, it will undoubtedly be steeped in conventions I was raised on in my five decades as a white cisgender woman who grew up in Northern California. So, while writing, I keep in mind what Matthew Salesses says in his book, *Craft in the Real World: Rethinking Fiction Writing and Workshopping,* that "We must be careful not to frame craft as prescription or even guidelines without first making it clear where those guidelines come from and whom they benefit. In many workshops, in many craft books, the dominance of one tradition of craft, serving one particular audience (white, middle-class, straight, able, etc.) is essentially literary imperialism, a term that should make us wary of the danger especially to emerging minority and marginalized voices."

Which is to say that if anything does not resonate with you for one of these reasons, trust *yourself*, not me.

What Is Tone?

We've touched on voice, but what about tone? If voice is like the personality and influences of your character leaping off the page, then tone is how you want people *to feel* when they read your book, scene by scene and in its final crescendo. Tone is the mood lighting and camerawork that sets the reader up for an experience. Tone is the shadow of flames that lick the pages as you read. It's sparks of fury or an icy scolding. It's the poetry of someone's pain felt in the reader's bones, or the great guffaw that humor can leave on the page.

This book will unpack, with numerous contemporary examples, some of the mysteries of voice and tone (also see: style) so fiction and nonfiction writers alike can wield them intentionally, finding and honing your voice and that of your characters, improving your chance of publication and connecting you more deeply to your work.

It will also briefly touch upon the power and value in voice for each of us and the way voices can and should evolve.

A Rain of Voice

Before we dive into particulars and mechanics, I'd like to present you with a series of different voice excerpts across genres. As you read each one, let voices fall over you like rain. Let them course through you, buzz, and vibrate. Let them speak of their ancestry. Let them chorus, let them clang. Find resonance, cringe at their discordance, feel moved to whoop or shout through their pain.

As you read each excerpt, also consider some questions. How would you characterize this voice? What does this voice know? What does it want? Where is it from and what has it been through? Does it draw you in like a swift current? Does it make music? Does it shout, preach, invite, tease? What do you feel before you even know anything about the character, the narrator? What feeling, mood, or attitude does it lay down? Does it stop you cold, invite you into a warm dance, or do something else altogether?

Don't worry so much about what it is yet; just enter each one:

> Once upon a time people said some babies here are born with their heads too big or with too many of them, skin searing off and eating itself. The group of men who own everything in this town—the casino, the tannery, the old fishery, and the newspaper—say it's all good. Nobody's dying. Nobody has a baby with a head too big or born with too many of them. Everyone's skin is shiny, intact, and not slowly eating itself.
>
> —*Tannery Bay*, a novel by Steven Dunn and Katie Jean Shinkle

* * *

INTRODUCTION

On the path ahead, stepping out from behind a boulder, a man appears.

We are, he and I, on the far side of a dark tarn that lies hidden in the bowl-curved summit of this mountain. The sky is a milky blue above us; no vegetation grows this far up so it is just me and him, the stones and the still black water. He straddles the narrow track with both booted feet and he smiles.

—I AM, I AM, I AM: SEVENTEEN BRUSHES WITH DEATH, A MEMOIR BY MAGGIE O'FARRELL

* * *

This is what I know: She left last night. My mother, Billie Jean Fontaine, stood in our front hallway with a stale cigarette in one hand and her truck keys in the other. The light in our hallway was broken or dying so it flickered above her head, throwing shadows across her face. I don't know how long she was standing there watching me.

I was only feet away on the couch in my nightpants trying to arrange my body like the woman in the Whitesnake video. It was not going well.

—HEARTBREAKER, A NOVEL BY CLAUDIA DEY

* * *

I did not want to write to you. I wanted to write a lie. I did not want to write honestly about black lies, black thighs, black loves, black laughs, black foods, black addictions, black stretch marks, black dollars, black words, black abuses, black blues, black belly buttons, black wins, black beens, black bends, black consent, black parents, or black children. I did not want to write about us. I wanted to write an American memoir.
I wanted to write a lie.

—*Heavy*, a memoir by Kiese Laymon

* * *

"You don't have to love him, just make his baby," Mama said, hanging the fleshy swath of salmon to dry. "It might have colored eyes, you know, maybe blue eyes. He'll pay you to keep quiet about it."

Mama had always been Machiavellian, but this was next level. Not even the old ladies who gossiped about her would have guessed she'd try to pull something like this.

—"Kushtuka," a short story by Mathilda Zeller in the anthology *Never Whistle at Night* edited by Shane Hawk and Theodore C. Van Alst Jr.

* * *

INTRODUCTION

> Rotating about the earth in their spacecraft they are so together, and so alone, that even their thoughts, their internal mythologies, at times convene. Sometimes they dream the same dreams – of fractals and blue spheres and familiar faces engulfed in dark, and of the bright energetic black of space that slams their senses. Raw space is a panther, feral and primal; they dream it stalking through their quarters.
>
> —ORBITAL, A NOVEL BY SAMANTHA HARVEY

While this book considers that readers may sort themselves into fiction and nonfiction writers, there's likely a little bit of something for everyone in each of its pages. Let's dive in!

"I'm most interested in character. However, character is informed by culture, and culture is informed by environment."

—N.K. JEMISIN

CHAPTER 1

Voice Emerges from Backstory and History

Backstory Shapes Voice

It barely needs saying that experience shapes us at multiple levels. Literature itself is steeped in the exploration of these influences and history on a character or narrator. What's noteworthy for *this* book is how those influences shape character or narrator voice and tone. In fiction, we call everything that has happened to the character prior to the start of the book "backstory," while in memoir / essay, it might just be called history (and the "voice of innocence," as we'll discuss in Chapter 6). However, "backstory" is also a useful catchall phrase that includes influences such as geography, culture, time period, social issues, family, and many more forces that shape your narrator or character.

This chapter will explore how those different influences seep out of the seams of character and enter voice, and how to be sure you're considering as many of these relevant influences as possible when crafting or curating your voice.

Family and Cultural Influences

Perhaps the two most immediate influences on any person in early childhood are family and cultural forces. Culture is a word flung around liberally in phrases from *company culture* to *local culture*, but let's run on the sociological meaning that culture describes a shared or agreed-upon set of beliefs, behaviors, customs, norms, values, etc., of a given society, group, or institution. Let's call *culture* an overview, an umbrella term, because within it is also the more accurate though often misunderstood term *subculture*.

For example, I always stumble when I try to drill down the culture of the United States, which some might call *American* culture, even though the Americas encompass numerous countries, from Canada up north all the way down to Chile in the south. Say your character's voice is steeped in the humid summers, complex history, and vocal twang of "the South" in the United States. Both Texas and Louisiana are considered the South, but I guarantee the "Southern" culture of each state has unique differences, not only in things like dialect, but influences, and those differences may get even more regionally exquisite the deeper you plumb.

VOICE EMERGES FROM BACKSTORY AND HISTORY

I can say I was steeped in "California culture"—and I certainly make fun of some of the attributions of the Northern California burbs where I grew up, steeped as they were in the leftovers of my parents' hippie-esque era, where my peers had names like Whisper and Cosmo, and health food was a religion. Yet someone living in an agricultural community with more conservative leanings likely has a totally different experience of the "culture of California."

And let's not forget that the United States is founded on the land of indigenous Americans, many of whom were not only stripped of their land and homes but their language and culture too, yet those tribal cultures and their voices persist.

I also delight in the dual meaning of *culture* in the language of microbiology, a way to grow organisms; that also seems to apply when you think of your character / narrator as uniquely grown in the substrate of their own specific influences. Thus, I urge you to dig deeply when looking at character / narrator culture to shape voice.

Before we go further, I'd like to offer two important thoughts on culture, as well: Another reference from Matthew Salesses's book *Craft in the Real World*, in which he challenges the canon of writing craft instruction for its tendency to frame a white, male, cisgender framework as the norm, or "literary imperialism," which often disregards the panoply of nuances that exist across cultures and genders, to name a few.

He writes, "Craft is not innocent or neutral. When I participate in the sharing and changing of craft, I can only do so by acknowledging my own attraction to certain cultural conventions. Culture stands behind what makes many craft moves 'work' or not, and for whom they work. Writers need to understand their real-world relationship to craft in order to understand their relationship to their audience and to their writing's place in the world. There's a lot of work left to do to open up craft to writers beyond the cis, straight, white, able, middle-class (etc.) literary establishment, and there is no 'pure' way of doing that work. There is only our engagement with culture."

In other words, don't assume your voice or craft approach is the only one or the norm, and it's also okay to write to your intended audience, who might be people with your shared set of experiences or culture and less like some "universal standard."

Secondly, on the topic of cultural appropriation. While artists and writers often argue that they should be able to use imagination to enter *any* culture or experience, those with lived experiences will tell you that it can sometimes be harmful. I like to fall on the side of sensitivity and consideration, of doing the least harm. At the minimum, hire a sensitivity reader for experiences vastly out of your own (particularly around race, gender, disability, and so on); at best, consider whether you are the right person to tell a story, particularly if it is of a group of people whose own voices have historically been (or are still being) systemically silenced, marginalized, or punished for speaking out. Ultimately, realize that any "culture" you choose to write from that is not your own reserves the right to pass judgment on you in ways you might not like.

Family

As we discuss culture, it's also important to look at *family*, which has its own culture within a culture: secrets sewn into hushed conversations or never spoken at all; traditions laid out with ceremony, meals, or decoration; behaviors or habits that may only make sense or serve a purpose to an "inner circle." The literature of psychotherapy is riddled with the complications of family culture, though I'm not suggesting all family culture is bad or dysfunctional; instead, I'm hoping you'll mine it for its complexities and uniqueness in shaping voice.

Let's start by diving into some examples of how culture and family culture shape voice.

Millions of readers were taken with the voice of Little Dog, the narrator from Ocean Vuong's epistolary novel *On Earth We're Briefly Gorgeous*, which reads like a memoir (and is sometimes referred to as "auto-fiction," or fiction that's based on fact). It's written as a series of letters from a son to his mother as he unpacks their traumas related to their home country of Vietnam, their immigration to the

United States, and other issues of violence, identity, and expression. Every time you read a passage in this book, I hope you'll pause for a moment and think about what kind of voice this is, the intimacy or distance it allows you from the character's experience, what you know, or what questions it leaves you with.

> Content note: Child abuse

> The first time you hit me, I must have been four. A hand, a flash, a reckoning. My mouth a blaze of touch.
> The time I tried to teach you to read the way Mrs. Callahan taught me, my lips to your ear, my hand on yours, the words moving underneath the shadows we made. But that act (a son teaching his mother) reversed our hierarchies, and with it our identities, which, in this country, were already tenuous and tethered. After the stutters and false starts, the sentences warped or locked in your throat, after the embarrassment of failure, you slammed the book shut.

This is a voice recounting pain, but it's not martyred voice; it is understanding. This son, no matter his pain, seems to have an inherent understanding at the root of his own suffering. He is making poetry out of his pain in the words, "My mouth a blaze of touch." He knows why his mother behaved as she did in the phrase "reversed our hierarchies" because he can see their identities as immigrants, "were already tenuous and tethered."

VOICE EMERGES FROM BACKSTORY AND HISTORY

We are introduced to a voice that is poetic in its truth-telling; not harsh, condemning, or judgmental. The voice is honest and vulnerable, and one that I as a reader really trust.

But perhaps what makes Little Dog able to be so tender toward the mother who also hurts him is that he knows some of *her* backstory, as recounted here:

> Because I am your son, what I know of work I know equally of loss. And what I know of both I know of your hands. Their once supple contours I've never felt, the palms already callused and blistered long before I was born, then ruined further from three decades in factories and nail salons. Your hands are hideous—and I hate everything that made them that way. I hate how they are the wreck and reckoning of a dream.

Little Dog's voice is lyrical and full of imagery, which softens the edges of pain. He could have written much more directly and even judgmentally about their experiences, yet this voice yearns toward compassion.

Or here, let's entertain a character's family history that strikes a very different tone as she recounts a detail from her own history. Our protagonist, Gail, in Teri Bayus's novel *The Greatest of Ease: A Circus Story*, literally runs away with the circus:

> They call me Gail or "Shit for Brains." I was born as a result of a whiskey hard-on in the backseat of a rusting

Pontiac on prom night in 1961. I was never supposed to amount to anything, so I tried everything.

Similar to Little Dog in Vuong's novel, Gail doesn't appear to feel sorry for herself about how she came to be or fear any external judgments that might be passed upon her. "I was never supposed to amount to anything…" If anything, she almost wears it as a badge: "so I tried everything." This voice sounds fearless, unafraid to tell it not only like she thinks it is, but in ways that might not necessarily be flattering. She's real and raw.

Historical Time Period

All these backstory elements can (and should) vary based on your story's time in history. If your characters live in a century or decade when women or people of color had no agency, power, or voice, for example, then the ways their voices come through on the page will be different from similar characters set in modern circumstances where they do have that agency.

For example, From Tananarive Due's novel *The Reformatory*, set in the Jim Crow South of the 1950s, a time when Black folks lived segregated lives from whites, the characters' lives and voices are informed by the continued insults and onslaughts of racism.

Sixteen-year-old Gloria Stephens lives alone with her little brother Robbie after their father flees town for his life after being accused of assaulting a white woman, and their mother has died of cancer. One day, on their way to a local swimming hole, they encounter Lyle McCormack, the son of a moneyed and feared white man in town. He makes a pass at Gloria, and her brother Robbie defends her, kicking him. In a normal setting, a young boy kicking a slightly older boy would earn nothing more than chastisement. But Robbie is Black in a racist social order, and Lyle is white—it could mean violence, even death for Robbie. I've cribbed bits of the dialogue to show how the time period and the racism shape the characters' experience; thus, voice:

> For an amazed instant, Robert thought he meant to kiss her—but instead, he whispered in a voice just loud enough for Robert to hear, "You look nicer'n those gals at Pixie's."
>
> Gloria stared at him with a moon-eyed face Robert had never seen on his sister, so childlike it frightened him.
>
> Lyle McCormack grinned. "You can do more'n scrub floors, Glo, I know you can."
>
> Then he winked at her …
>
> "Leave her be!" Robert said.
>
> Lyle's eyes dropped down to him. "What's got into you?"
>
> Gloria backed up a step behind Robert, but Robert remained fixed, a wall.
>
> "Move, Robbie," Lyle said, and shoved him aside, so

much power in the blunt motion that Robert stumbled two steps. His upper arm smarted from the heel of Lyle's hand.

"Stop it!" Gloria said to Robert. "Mind your business."

But Robert ran toward Lyle McCormack, swinging his foot at the bigger boy's left knee, and his new boot's bulk sank into the side of Lyle's kneecap with a thunk of bone.

...

"He didn't mean it, Lyle," Gloria said. "He's stupid! It's just me looking after him since Mama died. He don't have his daddy now either." Gloria was talking fast, as if Lyle McCormack were holding a shotgun to his head.

Lyle's voice is entitled and mildly threatening. In this scene, due to the inherent threat of violence or retribution, Gloria must reject her innate truth and the ability to speak it, so she's all but muted here. She can't shrug off Lyle's advances easily without offending him, and she can't allow her brother to stand up for her. When she does speak, she lies, calling her brother stupid, when she, and the reader, knows he's anything but.

A modern-day Gloria might just tell him to "watch his mouth," or to "back the fuck up," but 1950s Gloria doesn't have this permission.

Other Social Influences

If we return to the microbiologic definition of culture as a kind of substrate in which to grow something, then the world around your character and its many social influences are important parts of that growth. However, "social influences" is such a wide category, it's like saying "food" to describe someone's diet. Social influences emerge from and are connected to cultural influences and time period, geographic location, and more. It's important to consider the ways these might be shaping your character, and thus their voice or method of communication.

For example, there are some definitive generational differences in the way people use social media. Millennials and younger either grew up with early access to the internet or were born "digital natives"—after the internet was an inherent part of life. One of the things I often have to point out in my manuscript edits to baby boomers and Gen Xers is that younger characters in contemporary times are generally fluent with social media, and if your characters neither interact with nor are familiar with at least one form of social media or technology or another, it will read as implausible (unless you've got a good reason: say, a character raised off the grid).

Social media informs adult lives and voices too. In Naomi Alderman's speculative novel, *The Future*, set in the not-too-distant future, Martha Einkhorn, an adult white woman, is the daughter of a former cult leader who now works as an assistant for a billionaire social media tech guru named Lenk Sketlish. Martha's history of surviving a sociopath like her father has uniquely poised her to work for a man like Lenk. Martha is coming to the realization that billionaires of this sort are hell bent on keeping up their planet-ruining gains while they build comfortable bunkers for the end times. She undertakes a project that is largely the focus of the novel (no spoilers). Martha adopts the username OneCorn in a social media platform called the "Name the Day," a survivalist forum where she recasts the biblical stories of her religious-cult childhood to sow ideas for social change. When she is inhabiting her online persona, her voice is shaped by the expectations and conventions of both the medium of the forum and the times she's living in.

Soooo ... who's up for a little ... Bible Study?

I am on my interesting historical lessons, thank you.

Burning is the inevitable fate of anyone who tells people stuff worth hearing. Believe me. Today's lesson is on the theme: When is it time to go?

It's not not about billionaires owning intense survival bunkers.

No one has ever been able to stop you hating on Lenk Sketlish, AM. But yeah. This is relevant. It's about very powerful people and it's about social responsibility. OK?

Alright.

VOICE EMERGES FROM BACKSTORY AND HISTORY

> Genesis chapter 18, loosely translated.
>
> CW: sexual assault, murder, destruction of property, explosions, terror, incest, rains of fire, pillars of salt, violent death, Blasphemy, God.
>
> So the Lord looked at Sodom and it was not a great place to live, work, or raise a family. The people of Sodom were cruel, they took whatever they wanted, they had stopped caring for strangers or the poor. They were genuinely disgusting.

Martha's adopting a casual voice and tone here, translating a biblical story into language that this forum can hear—for example, the "CW" stands for "content warning," a habit adopted in recent years that lets people know what kinds of upsetting content might be forthcoming. Nobody would normally think to do that for the Bible—she's a product of her times. Additionally, her history growing up in a cult and her understanding of how people process information online all shape the "voice" she uses as OneCorn.

Trauma

If experience shapes character, traumatic experiences do so in even more intense ways. Trauma has been shown to do more than leave bad memories; it can stress and impede development in children and increase adverse mental and physical outcomes in adults. Whether this is childhood trauma or any garnered in adult life, it's an undeniable force that many people have some experience with.

If your characters are forged in trauma, it will likely shape some aspect of their voice, particularly childhood trauma and painful experiences. But how that trauma manifests as voice does not always have to be dark and bleak. As Ocean Vuong showed us earlier, trauma can turn lyrical or even humorous (like gallows humor). Here are a couple of examples of the way trauma shapes voice in different experiences, fiction and memoir both.

Let's look at another example from Lucy Grealy's *Autobiography of a Face*, a memoir of the author's experience with childhood cancer and the disfiguring effects of multiple surgeries.

"I had cancer?"

"Of course you did, fool, what did you think you had?"

"I thought I had a Ewing's sarcoma."

"And what on earth do you think that is?"

"My family seemed rather incredulous, but it was true. In all that time, not one person ever said the word cancer to me, at least not in a way that registered as pertaining to me.

It was as if the earth were without form until those words were uttered, until those sounds took on decisions, themes, motifs. There may have been thousands, millions of words uttered before those incisive words, but they had no meaning, no leftover telltale shapes to show that they had existed.

VOICE EMERGES FROM BACKSTORY AND HISTORY

Grealy's voice here turns the bewilderment of pain into metaphor, into poetry in the phrase beginning, "It was as if the earth were without form until those words were uttered…" In doing so, she shows us how something as simple as naming the source of her trauma—in this case, cancer—shaped her experience of herself and the world.

In another example, from Gillian Flynn's thriller *Dark Places*, protagonist Libby Day, the sole survivor of a murdered family, has a voice that is not self-pitying or sad, but something else:

> I have a meanness inside me, real as an organ. Slit me at my belly and it might slide out, meaty and dark, drop on the floor so you could stomp on it. It's the Day blood. Something's wrong with it. I was never a good little girl, and I got worse after the murders.

And another passage:

> I was not a lovable child, and I'd grown into a deeply unlovable adult. Draw a picture of my soul, and it'd be a scribble with fangs.

For me, Libby's voice is wry and sardonic—she's already thought all the worst things about herself that others might say, so there's no judgment anyone could impart that could be worse.

Finally, I was recently taken with the voice/s from the pathos-laden and largely uncategorizable novel *Big Swiss*, by Jen Beagin. The character dubbed "Big Swiss" (real name Flavia, initials FEW) has had an incredibly traumatic experience, but does not hold onto her trauma and can discuss it in a very dispassionate manner. Greta is the transcriber who works for Big Swiss's therapist, dubbed "OM" in the transcripts, and is *very* attached to her own trauma. This scene is from Greta's POV as she transcribes it—hence her interjections—and it follows the scene after which Big Swiss has detailed her traumatic experience to OM, without much emotion.

> OM: I wonder if you'd be interested in doing some chanting with me.

"Dear god in heaven," Greta said.

> FEW: What sort of chanting?

> OM: I was thinking we could chant the word "Har," which is another word for God.

> FEW: You're joking, right?

"You wish," Greta said.

> OM: "Har" is an ancient mantra for prosperity and good health.

> FEW: We'll be repeating the word "Har"? As in, "har, har, har"?

> OM: You'll be surprised how you feel afterward. "

You'll feel homicidal," Greta said.

> OM: I can start us off, and you can join in if the spirit moves you.

FEW: Okay.

OM: I'll put on some music. [CHANTING MUSIC]
OM: Raise your arms above your head at about sixty degrees, palms facing out. Good. Curl your fingers toward your palms, but leave your thumbs free. That's right, like that. [HAR HAR HAR HAR HAR]

The chanting went on for three excruciating minutes, during which Greta strained to hear Big Swiss, but of course Om drowned her out, as he was practically shouting.

OM: How do you feel?

FEW: How am I supposed to feel?

OM: Well, I feel totally cleansed of mental chatter. What about you?

FEW: Vaguely angry.

"Told you," Greta said.

Though both characters express themselves differently, there's humor in both voices—Big Swiss's is a dry humor, Greta's punchier. I love the tension between the characters' different ways of relating to painful experiences, and the unique differences in their voices.

Regional / Geographic Influence

Lastly, but not even remotely least, consider things like regional or geographic influence on your characters' voices. This is another reason why it's important to be very careful when writing characters from a region you haven't personally experienced—it's all too easy to work in idioms, accents, and phrases that folks in that area wouldn't use.

Here's an example from Alisa Lynn Valdés's thriller, *Hollow Beasts*. In it, a bilingual, Hispanic game warden is calling out a white poacher she's caught in the act in New Mexico, a place that is rich in cultures, and where more people speak Spanish than don't:

> Content note: Racism

> "Why the hell can't you Mexicans simulate like everybody else? You want to speak Spanish, go back to Mexico."

> "The word you're looking for is 'assimilate,' Travis," said Jodi, staring him down with equal and greater anger than he had. "Some people might find it ironic that a man who cannot master the English language is lecturing a fully bilingual woman, with several published books in that language, about how she is supposed to speak English."

You can mine backstory for voice. The goal is to dial it all down to some consistent habits, quirks, turns of phrase, manners of expression, and more, which we'll see as we continue reading.

Your character's voice is shaped by so many elements of experience, time period, place, and the people who influenced them. Whether or not you make these overt to the reader, as long as you know them, they can help you intentionally shape character voice.

In Summary

- **Backstory shapes voice:** A character's backstory—including family, culture, historical period, and geography—influences the voice and tone of your story. Mine it for rich detail.

- **Culture vs. subculture:** Culture encompasses a shared set of beliefs and behaviors within a group, while subcultures offer more specific and unique nuances. Consider your characters' deeper layers of cultural identity in shaping voice.

- **Family dynamics:** Family culture can also play a key role in shaping a character's voice, with secrets, traditions, and unspoken rules creating unique expressions and perspectives.

- **Time period matters:** The era in which a character lives impacts their voice. Historical and social contexts such as race relations, gender roles, and societal constraints, determine how characters speak and what they can say.

- **Social influences and technology:** The generational and social environment, including access to technology like social media, influences a character's voice. For instance, characters from different time periods or social backgrounds may use vastly different forms of communication.

- **Trauma's influence:** Traumatic experiences can shape voice, often resulting in complex and multilayered expressions.

- **Regional / geographic influences:** Geographic location impacts voice, as regional idioms, accents, and local vernacular shape how characters communicate. Writing characters authentically requires understanding and respect for these influences.

- **Sensitivity and appropriation:** Writers should approach cultural representation with care, considering the impact of their own background on how they portray voices from different cultures or marginalized groups, and being mindful of cultural appropriation.

VOICE LESSONS

Writing Exercises

Now, you give it a try!

Family or Childhood Influences

Write a scene in which your character tells a story from their childhood or family to someone who has no idea about what they've been through. Without explicitly stating what their upbringing was like, let their tone, vocabulary, and the details they focus on reveal what kind of experience it was and how it shaped them.

Culture

Write a monologue or internal reflection in which your character struggles to express something deeply personal due to cultural influences. This could be a character from a reserved culture struggling to express something personal or intimate, or a character from a storytelling tradition using metaphor and parable instead of direct language. Pay attention to sentence rhythm, word choice, and indirect communication.

Historical Period

Write a letter, journal entry, or dialogue in which your character expresses frustration about something that is holding them back. Try to shape their voice through the language, idioms, and worldview of their historical time period. Try to lean into what would have been normal phrasing and concerns for their era.

Social Influences

Write a scene in which your character must speak to a group of people with whom they are not in the same social circles. This could be generational differences, socioeconomic differences, or a person at the lower end of a company having to speak to their CEO, for example. What do they hold back or exaggerate? How do they feel?

Trauma

Write a dialogue-heavy scene in which your character is triggered by something subtle—a smell, a phrase, a gesture—and their tone shifts drastically. Maybe they become curt and withdrawn, or overly defensive and loud. Try to show their trauma through the sound of their / your voice rather than explicitly stating what happened to them. If this is memoir or essay, please take good emotional care of yourself before and after.

Regional / Geographic Influence

Write a short descriptive passage in which your character describes their home. Use sensory details, metaphors, and, if appropriate, regional slang to shape their voice. Would a character from New Orleans describe a storm differently than one from the Arizona desert? Would someone from a small town narrate differently than someone from a big city? Let some emotion trickle out—if they love or hate where they're from, how might that change the tone?

> *"Surely it is a magical thing for a handful of words, artfully arranged, to stop time. To conjure a place, a person, a situation, in all its specificity and dimensions. To affect us and alter us, as profoundly as real people and things do."*
>
> —Jhumpa Lahiri

CHAPTER 2

Voice Is Created Through Specificity of Imagery and Detail

Voice Is in the Specifics

An important element that differentiates one voice from another is *specificity*, uniquely chosen aspects of a character's or narrator's identity, perspective, phrasing, and conception of reality. Specificity lives in all the personal choices a character or narrator makes, and the intentional details of the world you reveal around them in a scene. And remember that voice is not just manifest in the spoken word, but in thoughts, actions, and feelings, as well.

When we get into the mechanics of voice at the sentence and word-choice level in Part Two, we'll look closely at the techniques you can use to intentionally create this detail. For now, let's look at it from the perspective of uniqueness and personality, of how characters who bring their detailed choices and observations to reveal voice are the ones we remember best. In this chapter, draw upon those backstory details from Chapter 1 to remind you who your characters / narrators are, and consider how this comes through in their voice.

A character who uses gallows humor to convey emotion, for example, will have a different voice from one whose voice is drawn from a career spent forcing their speech into the terse language of academia. A character steeped in the lyrical cadences of Louisiana will use different specifics from a character who spends most of their life surfing the Hawaiian Islands.

Imagery Specificity

Renowned writer Toni Morrison said that images provide a touchstone "to yield up a kind of truth." I love this idea of "a kind of truth," perhaps one that is interpreted by the reader. I am also a big fan of a lyrical or illustrative image. Images emerge from descriptive language that engages the senses and creates vivid mental pictures or sensations for the reader.

Images:

- Speak more to the unconscious mind through symbol, metaphor, simile, or other poetic or stylized language than they do plainly.

- Often bypass the conscious mind and cut straight to the heart and gut in the same way that poetry, divorced from standard sentence construction or using poetic tricks like juxtaposition and intentional rhythms, can.

- Can act like little "gems" or "bombs" in a sentence, communicating emotion and other personal flavors of character in an indirect but often even more powerful way than if you said something straightforwardly.

Here are a few:

"Their eyes were four huge hurting questions." (*The Need*, Helen Phillips.) The description of the children's eyes communicates fear and uncertainty without stating it outright.

"His voice was cloves and nightingales; it took us to spice markets in the Celebs. We drifted with him on a houseboat beyond the Coral Sea. We were like cobras following a reed flute." (*White Oleander*, by Janet Fitch) The voice's sensory descriptions suggest seduction and allure.

"What was it like to live with genius? Like living alone. Like living alone with a tiger." (*Less*, by Andrew Sean Greer) The voice is wry and sarcastic inside the sharp simile.

An excellent use of imagery for shaping unique character voice comes from Julia Heaberlin's lyrical crime novel *We Are All the Same in the Dark*. Here, we meet Wyatt, a character we know little about at the start, who has just discovered the body of a girl (alive!) on his property on a hot summer day in Texas.

> She has a bad, bad mystery to her. I can feel it deep in the hollow of my spook bone, the one my dad broke when I was a kid. My arm is never wrong. I poke her with the toe of my boot like I would any animal I thought was dead. An eye flutters open and closes. Not dead. Maybe half-dead. The heat's so bad out here the crickets are screaming for grace.

Wyatt's observational choices are charming, even though we don't know anything about him. There are many ways a character could say he's confused and alarmed to find a young girl half-conscious on his property. But having a "bad, bad mystery to her" immediately provides a sense of character and voice much different from "she made me nervous." Then, the clincher is his "spook bone," which readers can take to both literally mean a part of the arm (one his father broke, it's worth mentioning) and, figuratively, his sense of intuition. This use of imagery shapes a voice that is wholly unique.

Here's another one from Teri Bayus's novel *The Greatest of Ease*, in which protagonist Gail has literally run away from home to join the circus. She introduces herself to the reader:

VOICE IS CREATED THROUGH SPECIFICITY OF IMAGERY AND DETAIL

> I've learned in sixty years on the planet that I am a unicorn. I'm a left-handed, redheaded, blue-eyed creature. My blood is O negative, I only had two wisdom teeth, and I have an IQ of 185. I love instantly and completely. I'm fearless and will try anything once. I read so much; I pronounce everything wrong. I have no sense of time and no regard for money, and I dance like I'm on fire. Mostly, I've learned that happiness doesn't wrinkle.

What sense do you get of this person? Who is she, and what is she like? Why does she choose to tell us these specific details about herself?

The character clearly *feels* unique—she describes herself as a "unicorn," after all, that mythological creature and a term often used to signify something as rare or one of a kind. She cites things that are less genetically common, such as being left-handed, redheaded, and blue-eyed, as well as having O-negative blood. It feels as though the character is trying to get ahead of any judgments readers might bring to bear on her later by charming them with her best qualities up front. Perhaps the world has not seen these qualities in her so far and she'll be damned if anyone else misses them.

Specificity in Observation

Specific observations, as well as imagery, contribute to voice. Consider this excerpt from Charlotte McConaghy's *Once There Were Wolves*, about an Irish naturalist named

Inti who is involved in rewilding wolves to a part of the world where they've nearly gone extinct (and also a book about trauma). Inti describes her surroundings:

> I move lightly past the other crates to the back of the truck's container. The rolling door's hinges rasp as they let me free. My boots hit the ground with a crunch. An eerie world, this night place. A carpet of snow reaches up for the moon, glowing for her. Naked trees cast in silver. My breath making clouds.

This character could have merely said, "The dark feels scary. There's a lot of snow and the moon is full." But her observations contain specific ways of seeing this scene that are tied to her voice. "This night place," "a carpet of snow," "naked trees." I also love the use of sentence fragments to create a sense of hushed brevity, as she's trying to be both quiet and still as she tracks the wolves.

Another example from the novel *Big Swiss* by Jen Beagin, mentioned in Chapter 1, is full of wry, unique, specific voices. Transcriptionist Greta becomes obsessed with a therapist's client, whom she dubs "Big Swiss" (not a comment on weight, it's worth noting). Both Greta, whose character reads as neurotic and avoidant, and Big Swiss, who is direct, even confrontational, have incredible voices chock full of specific details in imagery that Beagin doles out seemingly effortlessly.

Look at a few specifics offered by Greta. When first hearing Big Swiss's voice, she describes it as having "a distinct tactile quality." She then says it's "a voice you could snag your sweater on, or perhaps chip one of your teeth, but it was also sweet enough to suck on, to sleep with in your mouth."

Big Swiss, on the other hand, when her therapist also comments on her voice as being "unusual," takes over the description, deadpan, and describes it as "... like a blade. When I pick out pastries at the bakery, it sounds like I'm ordering someone's execution."

These specific details are so rich and telling and full of wry humor.

Differentiating Characters

A common critique writers hear is that multiple characters sound too similar. Part of the work of voice is tapping into these unique details and specifics that differentiate people from one another. While it's certainly possible that two people with similar characteristics, especially those that share commonalities, *could* sound similar, the more differentiation on the page you can bring, the better.

For writers who struggle with this, it's helpful to think of two people you know who are vastly different from one another and ask yourself what it is that comes across as different in how they speak, think, and act. That can sometimes offer a template. Ideally, a reader should be able to tell who is talking just by reading the character's narrative voice, without any cues.

Below are two short excerpts of the two main characters, Clare and Henry, in Audrey Niffenegger's debut novel *The Time Traveler's Wife*.

While there are cues of who is who, you would probably have little trouble differentiating them as the story goes on. Let's look at them and then discuss why.

> *Clare:* I am standing in the Meadow. Ten minutes ago the sky was coppery blue and there was a heavy heat, everything felt curved, like being under a vast glass dome, all near noises swallowed up in the heat while an overwhelming chorus of insects droned.

> *Henry*: I'm in the back of a police car in Zion, Illinois. I am wearing handcuffs and not much else. The interior of this particular police car smells like cigarettes, leather, sweat, and another odor I can't identify that seems endemic to police cars. The odor of freakoutedness, perhaps.

Without knowing anything about voice, it's obvious these are two different people. How? Clare's voice is lyrical—she's drawn to a lovely image, visuals like a "coppery blue" sky that also feels like being "under a vast glass dome." Her sentences are longer, fluid, as though she has all the time in the world to sit and observe. It's unsurprising that Clare's character is also a visual artist.

Henry, on the other hand, often comes across as direct, pragmatic, focused on the moment at hand and his own survival, since his character continually travels through

VOICE IS CREATED THROUGH SPECIFICITY OF IMAGERY AND DETAIL

time without choice and wakes up wherever and whenever (and typically naked). While you could say it's the circumstances that dictate the voice—perhaps in his shoes, Clare would be less lyrical, and Henry could find his inner poetry—the effect creates some notable differences in voice.

Another great example of a book full of rich, unique, varied voices of character whose voices rely upon unique differences—and one of my recent favorite reads—is a novel called *Tannery Bay* by Steven Dunn and Katie Jean Shinkle.

Steven visited one of my classes and explained that in his and Katie Jean's writing process, they worked to get the story's narrative voice unified, so a reader couldn't tell which of them was writing it, while they took on individual character voices uniquely.

Here are a few of the character voices from the book:

> *Willie Earl:* All you gotta do is make the Owners convinced Anita's art is worth a lot of money, that Anita is the artist to watch out for in Tannery Bay…But, you gotta speak their language. You can't be cussing, and don't drop your g's at the end of words. Matter of fact, over-enunciate your g's, *and* your r's white people love that shit. Don't be saying shit like 'grinnin' like a opossum eatin a sweet tater' or 'finer than a frog hair split four ways.' Don't be calling them folks no gooseneck peckerwoods and slew-footed heffas and trout-mouth heathens—don't call them nothing but sir or ma'am."
>
> *Anita*: Anita never forgot the feeling of wrapping her tiny arms around that big woman's leather coat. Of

the cool, clean air whipping her floral headscarf. Of the feeling when they were engulfed in the forests at the top of the Hills, the romance of trespass, the wonder of love. Everything felt new then. Of Rocko's flannel on her breasts when they lay on top of each other and kissed and watched the sky turn from pink to charcoal, each star opening itself, crystalline, bright.

While Willie Earl's voice is delivered directly in dialogue, Anita's comes through in narrative voice, which can be read as her thoughts. Both characters' voices carry a musicality, but with distinct rhythms in their syntax. Delores's and Willie Earl's more gerund-heavy cadences have an energy that makes you want to dance around the room, while Anita's voice, with its longer, descriptive sentences, has the slow, swaying rhythm of a gentle ballad.

By the end of this book, you'll have a lot more tools with which to help you differentiate voices, such as experimentation with varying sentence lengths, rhythm, and vocabulary choices, but specific details are a great place to start.

Specific Choices and Descriptions

Specificity is also important in character and narrator choices, because it grounds them in personal touches and helps make them real to the reader. For example, they don't just "have a drink"—they toss back a tequila shot or savor a Dr. Pepper. They don't just "put on a sweat-shirt"—it's a threadbare purple Prince hoodie that their dead best friend gave them in college. They don't have a "front yard"—it's a riot of weeds and untended roses. They don't just love "music"—they are really into a rare kind of medieval chamber music or only listen to '90s rap.

When we talk more about narrative voice and authorial voice, we'll break down how some of these choices may belong to the narrative voice more than to the character, but either way, they contribute to the whole warp and weft of the character's ecosystem of voice.

Even character descriptions build voice in this manner. With a couple of specific details, you can introduce a character to the reader without any backstory:

> Mirrors showed me that I was a girl with a white-blond pigtail hanging down over one shoulder; eyebrows and lashes the same color, and one of those faces some people call "harsh" and others call "fine-boned."
>
> —Boy, Snow, Bird, A NOVEL BY HELEN OYEYEMI

> We left Sasha chopping vegetables in the kitchen. She looked the same—willowy figure, eyes narrowed against the sun, red hair gone pale with gray.
>
> —The Candy House, A NOVEL BY JENNIFER EGAN

> While my brother memorized stories of boy warriors—Hiawatha and Peter Pan—I preferred the Velveteen Rabbit, whose hero believes that love has made him

Real, until he meets a living rabbit. O, the pain of discovering that a thing is not what you thought it was!

—*Abandon Me: Memoirs*, by Melissa Febos

By incorporating specificity—both in imagery and in how characters filter their world through their unique perspectives—you deepen the authenticity of their voices and create memorable characters that stand apart.

In Summary

- **Voice and specificity**: A character's voice is shaped by their unique way of seeing the world, including their thoughts, feelings, and choice of language. The more concrete you can be, the more you shape voice.

- **Power of imagery**: Specific images can convey emotions indirectly, bypassing the conscious mind and creating a deeper connection with the reader.

- **Character-driven imagery**: A character's perspective on the world influences the imagery you use, helping to define their voice and personality.

- **Use observation to shape voice:** How characters observe and describe their environment reveals their personality and voice, with unique phrases adding depth.

- **Differentiate character voices:** Distinct voices for each character reflect their backgrounds, personalities, and experiences, making it clear who is speaking.

- **Specificity in detail:** Small, concrete details about a character's actions, appearance, or surroundings create a more authentic and memorable voice.

- **Character voice through language:** The words a character uses, from slang to regional expressions, play a key role in developing their voice and making them stand out.

VOICE LESSONS

Writing Exercises

Now, you give it a try!

Character-Specific Voice

STEP 1: DEFINE THEIR VOICE

Before rewriting, gather key aspects of your character's voice:

- Five words or phrases they frequently use. (Such as: "reckon," "nope," "to be honest")

- Two defining personality traits that shape their tone. (Such as: sarcastic, anxious, dreamy)

- One strong opinion they hold that influences how they interpret the world. (Such as: "People who are always late can't be trusted.")

- Any slang, jargon, or speech patterns that reflect their background. (Technical jargon, regional expressions, clipped sentences).

VOICE IS CREATED THROUGH SPECIFICITY OF IMAGERY AND DETAIL

STEP 2: REWRITE WITH VOICE IN MIND
Using the details above, rewrite these neutral sentences in your character's distinct voice:

- "It was a bad day." How would your character phrase this? Would they be dramatic? Understate it? Make a joke?

- "The crowd was overwhelming." Do they find crowds exciting or suffocating? What sensory details would they notice?

- "The woman looked mad." How would they describe anger? Would they focus on body language, tone, or something unexpected?

- "It was the best thing that had happened." Would they express joy outright or downplay it? What comparisons might they use?

Replacing Vagueness with Character-Specific Details

We'll explore vagueness more in Chapter 11, "Cutting Clutter," but for now, let's practice sharpening details to make your character's voice more vivid.

STEP 1: IDENTIFY VAGUE ELEMENTS

Choose a scene from your manuscript and find three to five instances where a vague description could be made more specific to reflect your character's personality, background, or mood. Look for:

- Generic nouns (food, drink, clothes, car, book, music)

- Broad descriptions (big, nice, weird, interesting, bad)

- Unspecified emotions (She was happy.)

VOICE IS CREATED THROUGH SPECIFICITY OF IMAGERY AND DETAIL

STEP 2: MAKE IT SPECIFIC

Rewrite each vague instance with precise, character-driven details:

- Instead of "She ate a meal," try "She tore into a plate of greasy fish tacos, licking salsa from her thumb."

- Instead of "He put on his shoes," try "He laced up a brand-new pair of scuff-free white Adidas, careful not to crease the leather."

- Instead of "The room smelled bad," try "The air reeked of burnt coffee and yesterday's sweat."

STEP 3: REPEAT

If you really want to push your writing, repeat this process for every scene in your manuscript. Every detail is an opportunity to reinforce voice, deepen character, and make your world feel more real.

"There is a voice inside me, which I suppose is my voice but which I hear as if it's someone else's, the voice that says the words in my head when I read. My relationship to this voice is so intimate, so perfect, that most other people's voices feel like intrusions."

—Amy Bonnaffons, *The Regrets*

CHAPTER 3

Voice in Emotional Expression

Voice Is Expression

So much of what makes readers respond to and love a character's voice is steeped in emotion—from the raw and vulnerable to the fierce and confrontive. Voices that allow us to *feel* are often the most memorable.

However, emotion isn't just about characters laughing or crying; it encompasses a much broader spectrum. What truly defines a character's emotional depth is not only what they feel, but how they express it—the words they choose, the rhythm of their speech and thoughts, and the unique ways they reveal their inner world.

In this chapter, we'll explore emotion and expression as they relate to voice. We'll consider such questions as how your character responds under stress, whether they're defensive or self-aware in a confrontation, and their overall manner of expression (stoic, vulnerable, etc.).

When it comes to consciously shaping character voice, looking at our characters' emotional depths can help enhance voice. (It's also worth noting that a character who has little to no emotional access can still have a great voice—and we'll talk about that too.)

Emotional Coping Mechanisms

We all know people whose emotions are a little louder than other people's. Their grief or joy gushes forth in gouts of expression. Unafraid to wail or rail, these folks do more than allow an emotion—they live it. You also probably know others on the opposite end, whose emotions seem frozen in stone, barely able to be chipped away under the direst of conditions.

Consider your characters or narrator now. Do they stuff and suppress what hurts them? Do they live out loud like our example above? Do they have a healthy relationship with their difficult feelings, or a dysfunctional one? What do they do with difficult feelings?

We'll look at examples of emotional expression in the following excerpts.

In the thriller *The Collective*, by Alison Gaylin, protagonist Camille's teen daughter was murdered, her killer never found. Camille believes she knows exactly who did it: a young, wealthy, white man of privilege her daughter was dating at the time, Harris Blanchard. Wracked by grief she is nowhere near healing, she attends a ceremony some months later where that young man is receiving an award. Notice how Camille handles her emotions in the scene.

> Waverly says, "The recipient of the Martha L. Koch Humanitarian Award this year is a young man who exemplifies public service," and that's when I finally catch sight of him, standing in the rear corner of the room, his golden curls slicked down, his parents sentries on either side of him. I'd recognize them anywhere.
>
> Harris Blanchard pulls a piece of paper out of his pocket and unfolds it. My gaze pings on his mother, just as she mouths, I love you, sweetie, and I have no fucks left to give. The word bubbles up in my throat and escapes as a shriek. "Murderer!" I start toward Harris Blanchard. I don't get far.

Now, contrast this wild, desperate woman and her voice with Camille's voice the rest of the time in the story (and note why she is this way):

> I'm not always this way. That is to say, nine-tenths of the time I'm calm and cool and going about my business. To keep the cocoon tight and the pain at bay, I take pills. In my old life, I had no anxiety that couldn't be cured by my weekly hot yoga class. Obviously, things have changed since then.

Before her daughter's death, Camille was not the kind of person who would shout, "Murderer!" in a public space.

Before, it only took some "weekly hot yoga" to keep her calm and cool. After, she is a feral creature, shaped by grief, and the only thing that keeps Camille calm is "pills." This is another good example of how experiences shape our characters, their manner of expression, and their voices.

Now, let's examine another character whose emotional expression shapes voice in a way that contrasts with Camille's—Gail again, from Teri Bayus's novel, *The Greatest of Ease*. Gail, facing immense personal struggles, joins the circus hoping for a fresh start. Instead, she encounters even more challenges, including being treated as an outsider even after marrying one of the acrobats. Her mother-in-law, whom she simply calls Mama, takes it upon herself to make Gail's life a living hell.

> Most everyone ignored me, but Mama was out to kill me. She loosened the single trapeze when she knew I was going to be on it. She took springs out of the trampoline and left mousetraps in my suitcase (which was still in the cat garage). Those are the things I knew of; I am sure there were many other booby traps that I eluded. She spit in my dish when I left it unattended and crossed herself when I entered the trailer. The woman hated me, but I didn't care.

And:

> I was so glad when she went to work with them. For a few moments, the dysfunction was abated, but that only made me uncomfortable. I was used to and reveled in drama.

What do you notice about how Gail copes emotionally with these challenges versus Camille above? Here's a woman literally trying to sabotage her at best, kill her at worst—loosening a trapeze, taking springs out of a trampoline, and more. And Gail's response? "I didn't care."

In fact, when the drama abates because Mama is away at work, Gail finds herself "uncomfortable" because she "reveled" in drama. It speaks to a woman who might, in fact, be so used to drama and danger that this is just another day in her life. To me, Gail's voice throughout the novel is one that dares you to underestimate her, that puts herself in your face, but not in a hostile way; if ever there were a character for whom the cliché "take the bull by the horns" was designed, it's Gail.

Now, here's a heart-rending example from Shannon Luders-Manuel's memoir *The Ones Who Love You*, a memoir of growing up biracial and often disconnected from her parents. In this passage, we get a look at what it's like when the emotions one wants to express must be checked or squelched.

> I stepped off the train to see Dad leaning against a wooden pillar like a man straight out of the Harlem Renaissance. He took off his newsboy cap to reveal a patchy head of hair made thin by discoid lupus. The hair that remained was grayer than just last year, and his face had faint red splotches, as if a child had painted it at a carnival with a small brush. Nonetheless, he

was still the Black Prince—his self-appointed nickname.

As we ambled across the light-rail tracks to get to the car, Dad yelled, "Watch out!"

I screamed and ran as fast as I could to the other side of the street, certain that I was about to be crushed under an oncoming light-rail car. Dad hooted and hollered from the middle of the tracks.

"Got you!" he said. "Woo, you were so scared!"

I tried to look angry, but a grin escaped my face to copy his. There was my dad. Not lying drunk on a bed. He was alive, laughing, joking.

I feel so much for the narrator of this memoir, a child who has often been estranged from her father, with whom she yearns for a close connection; a man who has struggled with alcoholism and kept important truths from her, yet whom she loves so much. You sense that she is suppressing her natural inclination here—to let her anger flow—in favor of "taking what she can get" from this brief time with her father when he is in a good mood and emotionally and physically present for her.

Lastly, here's an example of barely checked emotional coping from Amanda Jayatissa's thriller *My Sweet Girl*. We're in protagonist Paloma's inner monologue in a moment of frustration when she doesn't immediately get the information she wants.

There's a special place in hell for incompetent customer service agents, and it's right between monsters who stick their bare feet up on airplane seats and mansplainers. Fake hair, false smiles, synthetic blazers that pool around their middles while they tell you that yes, they would love to help you, and thank you for your patience, and no, sorry for the inconvenience caused but they can't seem to find your paperwork even if it punched them square in the jaw. I inhaled. Be nice, Paloma. Be kind.

My hands were trembling slightly, so I made sure they weren't on the table in front of me. I hate how they do that when I'm angry. I hate it when I'm angry. It makes it hard to think straight. And I needed to think straight right now.

If you had to qualify Paloma's ability to cope with stress here, what would you say? Does she seem patient or quick to anger? Here's a woman who, in the moment of one minor irritation, is already ticking off a list of *other* irritations. This makes her language harsh and judgmental. Customer service agents who can't get her what she wants are "incompetent." People who stick bare feet up on airplane seats are "monsters." People who do things she doesn't like are "fake" and she's already imagining punching them. Paloma's got an anger issue, and it even manifests in her physical body—her hands tremble, and she has to work hard to quell this rage. Contrast this with Gail, whose actual life is in danger above, and you see completely different manners of expression manifested in voice.

Character Cues

Now that we've touched upon the ways that different forms of emotional expression can manifest in voice, let's go a little further into defining expression and emotion as voice. Despite that voice sounds like it is only connected to the spoken word, it's communicated through many other mechanisms, and so is emotion. In my book *Writing the Intimate Character,* I explore how to convey a character's or narrator's emotions through a series of "character cues." These cues serve as unique "signatures" that contribute to the character's voice—essentially, the distinct qualities that express their inner world.

We won't walk through all these cues, but I wanted to note that several of these can also shape and contribute to voice.

The cues we'll discuss include:

- **Physical action cues:** Characters communicate emotion through actions and embodiment.

- **Sensory cues:** Sensory experiences are a powerful way to communicate basic, primal emotion without being explicit.

- **Dialogue dues:** Characters' emotions cause them to speak in certain ways.

- **Thought cues:** Characters think in ways that manifest emotion or mirror a prior emotional time.

Physical Action Cues

Sometimes there are no words for emotion, or a character is too emotional to speak them. Instead, they enact their emotions, and that conveys a lot about a character. Here's another example from Alisa Lynn Valdés's novel *Hollow Beasts*, in which Latina game warden Jodi Luna confronts a suspected poacher in New Mexico.

> Lee looked Jodi up and down like she was for sale and sucked his teeth to dismiss everything she had just said. "You done now, honey?"
>
> Jodi took her pistol out of the holster and, keeping it pointed down at the ground, stepped ever so slightly closer to Lee. Part of her knew that this was reckless, that her temper was getting the better of her, again.
>
> "Sobrina, no," said Atencio. "Vamos."
>
> She ignored her uncle, many years of pent-up rage from the classier versions of this same ignorance she'd faced in college and, later, academia, fueling her. She put her face up close to Lee's, then smiled in a cold and controlled way she could see finally scared him.
>
> "Despite my sweet disposition and appreciation for the important ecological role of bees, Travis, my name is not *honey*." She locked eyes with him and let him hear the click of her releasing the safety on her pistol. "It's Jodi. But only to my friends. For future reference, you can just call me Officer Luna, ma'am, or, as long as you're in *my* state, Agente Luna, Señora."

What I love about Jodi's body language in this scene is that it reflects her personality in the same way her speech and thoughts do, all contributing to her unique voice. Her body language is bold and unafraid, and so is her personality. She moves closer to the threatening man at first, and then even puts her face "up close to Lee's" and "smiled in a cold and controlled way." When she drops into her dialogue, "Despite my sweet disposition… my name is not *honey*," her voice is loud and clear. This woman is unafraid.

Contrast this with another passage from Ocean Vuong's novel, *On Earth We're Briefly Gorgeous*, in which the character Little Dog is on the school bus in a place where he doesn't feel safe:

> All around me the boys jostled each other. I felt the wind from their quick-jerked limbs behind my neck, their swooping arms and fists displacing the air. Knowing the face I possess, its rare features in these parts, I pushed my head harder against the window to avoid them.

The boys in *Gorgeous* also pose a threat to Little Dog, an immigrant child in a largely white community where there isn't a lot of acceptance of people who look different. However, he chooses the path of safety: "I pushed my head harder against the window to avoid them." (A little note here: I love how the consonance of "h"s in head / harder allows you to almost *feel* that head pressing action.)

Additionally, within the category of physical cues comes

what I call "embodiment"—in which the ways a character inhabits their body, either through internal experience or the author's description of them, contribute to voice. Through embodiment, we see how characters' physicality reveals their emotional state, inner struggles, and unique identity. Here are two examples from Alex Marzano-Lesnevich's true-crime memoir, *The Fact of a Body:*

> The architect boys are beautiful. Greg scales the pitched peaks of the roof. His friends climb high ladders over the windows. They cut through the air like dolphins through water ...

And:

> I stare into the yellow and will myself into flame, into dissolution.

In both, the physicality described—the boys moving fluidly and effortlessly through the air, the narrator's intense self-dissolution—connects body and emotion, hinting at their embodied experience. This conveys a visceral experience that contributes to voice.

And lastly, one of my favorite novels, Porochista Khakpour's *The Last Illusion*, offers this embodied description:

> There he was, just a mass of bones held together by broken filthy skin, squatting against walls of twisted wire that his limbs would fight against with each passing year...and the only nice thing in there, the one thing he could never have, feathers ...

Here, the character's physical form—broken, fragile, and fighting against his circumstances—reveals his suffering, his sense of imprisonment, and his yearning for something unattainable. This offers not just a description of his body but an essential part of his emotional experience, even indirectly.

Physical cues don't merely describe actions; they offer another dimension to voice, revealing aspects of character that don't come through spoken word or internal thoughts.

Sensory Cues

Sensory cues, or sensory images, are another way to ground your character's reactions and emotions in the body. These cues filter characters' perceptions of the world and their emotions through the senses—sight, smell, touch, hearing, taste. These avoid "telling" words and pull readers inside your character's experience, set a tone or a mood, and convey emotion.

From simple sensations that convey emotion, to more complex images, metaphor or simile, these cues are often loaded with the uniqueness that creates voice. Let's look at a couple of different kinds.

SCENT / SMELL

Scent is powerful in shaping, revealing, and creating voice, because it's viscerally connected to emotional experience and memory. There's a certain floor wax that drops me right back into childhood summers at my grandmother's New York apartment, my shoes squeaking along the tile. The smell of jasmine flowers conjures an idyll of warm summer days at the pool with my father before he remarried.

Below are two examples of scent imagery that also capture different voices. Again, notice the differences in voice between the authors' examples.

The first is from Erica Bauermeister's novel *The Scent Keeper*: "The scent was gorgeous, generous, set off by a series of synthetic surreal scents, bright as searchlights, precise as expertly manicured fingernails tapping against a table."

This passage is rich with precision and complexity, which aligns with the character of a perfumer. The language here also mirrors the character's unique relationship with scent, turning it into something almost personal, something with personality and voice. You can imagine this scent as a person—defined, deliberate, and carefully constructed.

Second, from Lidia Yuknavitch's novel *Thrust*: "'You diseased devil,' he spat, his breath like rotting apples."

Here, scent is used more bluntly, cutting straight to the emotional core. The comparison of breath to rotting apples evokes disgust, revulsion, and a deeper emotional bitterness. This imagery is visceral and contributes to the character's voice in a much more immediate, perhaps even hostile, way. The scent of rot mirrors the speaker's feelings of contempt or loathing.

In both examples, scent is more than a sensory detail—it's an extension of the characters' emotions and personalities. Through scent, we can sense who they are, what they value, and how they experience the world. These subtle cues enhance their voices, making them more distinct, more alive in the reader's mind.

TOUCH

If it seems like a stretch that the way a character engages in contact with others can contribute to voice, think about everything from violence to intimacy and understand the vast lexicon of body language and contact. A tender touch between two people can mean many different things, after all, from pity to comfort, just as violence can spring from sources like abuse and fear.

Below is an example from Lauren Beukes's novel *Broken Monsters*, which I'd qualify as horror-adjacent, but not quite straight horror; it also has supernatural elements and reads like a literary novel. In it, the villain, who can shape-shift, is able to bend and twist reality around his / its victims. He comes to his most recent victim not as an aggressor, but as something much softer. I love this use of the unexpected, the juxtaposition of something predatory with something beautiful, an evil that is not a cliché, full of lovely imagery:

> What is this?" she murmurs, leaning on the counter. Her legs feel weak.

> "A dream," he says, stepping up to her, cupping his hand behind the base of her head, under her hair, tilting her chin down, while a tropical jungle springs into bloom around her.

The villain's contact with the victim, a simple, intimate gesture of tilting her chin, carries a profound sense of power and manipulation, but it's framed by an otherworldly beauty. This paradox—where intimacy becomes a tool of control—adds a haunting quality to the character's voice. Lastly, the juxtaposition of the soft, personal touch with the supernatural bloom of the jungle creates a kind of unease. In this moment, the contact reveals not just the villain's power, but the chilling unpredictability of his nature, and contributes to the atmosphere of voice.

DIALOGUE CUES

Perhaps the easiest place to "find" voice if you struggle with it is in dialogue, the place where your characters speak for themselves. Some people find it's easier to channel character voice this way, and to hear all the syntactical magic of wordplay and mood as it flows off the tongue, through a text channel, or other variation. It can be easier to access the more relaxed, honest, raw versions of your characters this way (though, as we will discuss when we get to code-switching, it can also be the landscape of performance and persona).

One of my favorite recent characters is yet another

example from Julia Heaberlin's beautiful crime novel, *We Are All the Same in the Dark*.

What the reader soon learns is that Wyatt—he of the "spook bone"—is a misanthropic man in a small Texas town whose sister, Trumanell, went missing eleven years ago. Though no one can prove he killed her, and not everyone thinks he did, that suspicion has always lingered. Rather than trying to prove he's innocent, he seems to revel in the malevolence their suspicion gives him—it keeps people away. Here, his ex-girlfriend, Odette, now a cop, is coming out to his farm because she's heard a young girl has turned up on his property in bad shape. Every word of Wyatt's is a challenge, a refusal to give her what she wants in a sparky, tension-filled dialogue.

> "Odette, what a surprise." A smile cracks his face. "Back for seconds?"
>
> "Put up the gun. I have to do my job. I've got a tip and I need to follow it. If I don't, someone else at the station will. You should prefer it's me."
>
> He says nothing, still grinning. He's always been primal, both aggressor and protector, and the danger of not knowing which unnerves me every time. I'm well aware that my uniform squares everything off, rendering my body sexless …
>
> "I want to get this out of the way first. What happened last month was a mistake." The words rush out of my mouth. "It isn't happening again. Ever."

"What did you think I meant by seconds? I'm referring to the couple of squares of peach cobbler left."

"It was a mistake."

"Somebody saw a girl in your truck when you rode through town earlier," I continue steadily. "Do you have a girl out here, Wyatt?" I let my eyes flick to the dress on the line, drying into a brittle scarecrow.

"Are you jealous?" He unlatches the screen and pulls the door shut behind him. His body is thick and impenetrable ...

"What are you going to do, Odette?" He's issuing a challenge. He feels me wavering. Daddy told me never to come back to this town.

Another of my favorite characters in recent literature is Jordan Hennessey, a "dreamer" in Maggie Stiefvater's YA fantasy Dreamer trilogy. Her character can bring dreamt objects into reality. She's also a world-class art forger. Hennessey, who had a traumatic childhood, defends herself behind humor and sarcasm. She can be sharp, biting, ironic, and hilarious. But you can always feel the defense behind it. In the third book of the series, *Greywaren*, she has an exchange with an uptight art gallery / secret society of art dealers head named Jo Fisher:

"I thought you wanted a forger," Hennessy replied.

Jo gestured vaguely at the walls around them. "And I thought you wanted this."

"What every child dreams of: a rigged career in the arts."

"A child's guide to the economy, by Jordan Hennessy," recited Jo Fisher.

"Ow."

A little later in the conversation, Hennessy circles back and makes fun of Jo in the way that Jo made fun of her. While Jo may just be making fun, Jordan's tone is a little sharper, a bit more cutting. She doesn't enjoy being the target.

"We're really just a bunch of businesspeople trying to make the world run a little more smoothly while paying our mortgages," Jo said.

"Mortgage! You don't have a mortgage," Hennessy shot back. "You have a dead houseplant, a personal massager, and a two-year lease for a place you never sleep in."

Jo Fisher glared.

Hennessy smiled widely. She added, "A child's guide to adult relationships, by Jo Fisher."

"I think we've gotten off on the wrong foot," Jo Fisher said …

Lastly, I love this little exchange from Julia Armfield's novel *Our Wives Under the Sea*, in which the protagonist's biologist wife has returned from a sea excursion that went missing for some months. Since her return, the protagonist's wife is changing in alarming ways.

She doesn't know that the first time I noticed the change

in her skin, I was so alarmed that I called 111 and hung on the line for thirty minutes, only for someone to finally come on and ask if I'd ever heard of impetigo.

"You don't need to look at me like that," she says now, still moving her fingers along the skin of her arm. "I can feel your look," she adds when I open my mouth to say something. "But you don't need to. It's OK."

"I'm not looking at you in any special way," I say, in a voice that aims for a joke and misses.

She gives me a sideways look, starts to smile and then doesn't entirely.

"OK," she says. "So you're not looking at me. My mistake."

Their emotional exchange reveals a kind of passivity, barely concealing that neither wants to talk directly about what's happening, and so they are resorting to indirect expressions of emotion.

Dialogue is a straightforward method of expressing what a character feels. Sometimes characters just say what they're feeling in direct language. Other times, they speak *from* a place of emotion.

Think of the kinds of things your character might say in their given emotional state. When sad, do they get needy? When hurt, do they lash out in anger? What truths or authenticity might spew forth when they're emotional?

THOUGHT CUES

Finally, I want to touch upon thought cues, those internal reflections that reveal a character's or narrator's state of mind, mood, and emotions. Thoughts may reveal emotional states the character can't or won't say aloud or may be used privately to cheer or encourage oneself in an upsetting situation. Emotional thoughts might hark back to memories whose emotional content matches what the character is going through right then.

Here's an example from Alyssa Cole's thriller, *When No One Is Watching*.

> It isn't fair. I can't sit on my stoop and enjoy my neighborhood like old times. Even if I retreat to my apartment, it won't feel like home because Mommy won't be waiting upstairs. I sit trapped at the edge of the disorienting panic that strikes too often lately, the ground under my ass and the soles of my flip-flops the only things connecting me to this place. I just want everything to stop.

In this passage, protagonist Sydney's thoughts reveal loss and dislocation. The feeling of being "trapped at the edge of disorienting panic" conveys an immediate anxiety but also her deeper sorrow about the loss of her mother and the changes in town. As her grief and panic collide, her vulnerability and longing come through. I also like the way the use of sensory detail ("the ground under my ass and the soles of my flip-flops") plants the character's emotional turmoil in the physical reality of their environment.

One last thought example comes from Liz Michalski's novel *Darling Girl*, in which the legend of Peter Pan isn't a legend for the modern Darling family, but a sinister part of their history and success. Protagonist Holly Darling has been keeping a very big secret from even her closest friends and acquaintances, that she has a daughter named Eden who lives in a coma due to an accident that happened years before, and is cared for in her home back in England. In this scene, her assistant has just learned of Eden.

"Holly."

"Hmmm?" She doesn't look up.

"I really am so sorry. When was the last time you saw her? Eden, I mean."

She wants to say, *I see her every time I look in the mirror. Every night in my dreams. Every time I look at Jack.* But she doesn't. "January," she says instead. "I saw Eden this past January." *And her face was still as beautiful as the stars.*

Here, the thoughts about seeing her daughter "every time she looks in the mirror" and in the face of her son Jack, that Eden's face is "as beautiful as the stars" conveys a melancholy, but also undergirds a lyrical nature to Holly's voice, even in her thoughts.

Thoughts have the ability to expand upon voice that might be limited in dialogue, creating deeper character understanding and giving life to strong voice.

Emotionally Reserved or Withholding Characters

For every character who emotes out loud and with vivid expression, there is a quiet stoic, an introverted thinker, someone shy or discouraged from expressing themselves in a big, bold, or dramatic way. They may have terse manners of speech, speak less, and think more, or be very precise or intentional in their expression. I saved this section for the end so you can see which character cues are being used to show that reservation or withholding.

There are other reasons a character may hold back emotionally, as in Laura Dave's thriller *The Last Thing He Told Me*.

In it, Hannah is stepmom to sixteen-year-old Bailey. The book opens with her new husband of a year, and Bailey's dad, Owen, having disappeared and left only a cryptic note that says, *Protect her*. Bailey has not yet warmed to Hannah, and now they're thrust together into a confusing scenario. Note the way Bailey responds—or doesn't—to Hannah in a series of examples (we're in Hannah's POV):

> I smile at her, my phone cradled under my chin. I have been trying to reach Owen, unsuccessfully, the phone going to voice mail. Again. And again. "Sorry, I didn't see you there," I say. She doesn't respond, her mouth pinched.
>
> "Is that what smells?" she says. She wrinkles her nose,

just in case it isn't clear that the smell to which she is referring isn't one she likes. "It's the linguine that you had at Poggio," I say. She gives me a blank look, as though Poggio isn't her favorite local restaurant, as though we weren't there for dinner just a few weeks before to celebrate her sixteenth birthday.

Bailey gets in the car quickly. She drops into the driver's seat and buckles herself in. She doesn't say hello to me. She doesn't even turn her head to look in my direction. "Are you okay?" I ask. She shakes her head, her purple hair falling out from behind her ears. I expect her to make a snide remark— *Do I look okay?* But she stays quiet.

Bailey communicates a lot with Hannah but not verbally, using physical action cues, as in "She doesn't respond, her mouth pinched," or the "blank look" she gives Hannah, and not turning her head to look at Hannah in the car. When she does reply, it's often sarcastic or defensive, and reads like a frustrated teen in a tough emotional spot. Though Bailey's behavior does hurt her feelings, Hannah is patient because she is still the new stepmother and knows it's a rough time for a teenage girl, but she also finds herself working hard to win over the teen. In the premise of the story, they'll need each other as they try to find out what happened to Owen. Bailey's voice comes through as aggrieved and frustrated much of the time, but most of that is not even communicated in her dialogue cues.

In another example, from Alix E. Harrow's urban fantasy *Starling House*, protagonist Opal is a young woman raising her teenage brother in an impoverished Kentucky town. She has had a long fascination with a local manor known as Starling House. One day, Opal happens past the house and encounters "the heir" who lives there, a man so reserved and private, nobody knows anything about him. In this first exchange, we get this vision of the heir as terrifyingly terse, from her POV.

> "Oh, I didn't see you there!" I clutch my chest and give a girly little laugh. "I was just passing by and thought I'd take a closer look at these gates. They're so fancy. Anyway, I didn't mean to bother you, so I'll head on my way."
>
> The heir to Starling House doesn't smile back. He doesn't look like he's ever smiled at anything, actually, or ever will, as if he were carved from bitter stone rather than born in the usual way. His eyes move to my left hand, where the blood has soaked through the wadded sleeve to drip dramatically from my fingertips.
>
> "Oh, shit." I make an abortive effort to shove the hand into my pocket, which hurts. "I mean, that's nothing. I tripped earlier, see, and—"
>
> He moves so quickly I barely have time to gasp. His hand darts through the gate and catches mine, and I know I should snatch it back—when you grow up on your own from the age of fifteen you learn not to let strange men grab ahold of any part of you—but there's an enormous padlock between us and his skin is so warm and mine is so damn cold. He turns my hand

> palm up in his and I hear a low hiss of breath. ...
>
> He leans closer, forehead pressing hard against the iron, fingers wrapping whitely around the bars. My blood is slick and shining across his knuckles. "Run," he grates.
>
> I run.

Then, in the next scene, through thought cues, we discover a man with much more depth and range of emotion and possibly less menace than we thought when we first encountered him.

> The heir to Starling House watches her run from him, and does not regret it. He doesn't regret the way she ripped her hand from his, or the way her eyes flashed at him before she ran, hard and flat as beaten nails. He especially does not regret the sudden departure of that bright, bold smile, which had never been real in the first place. He wrestles with a brief, absurd urge to shout after her—wait, he might say, or maybe even come back—before he reminds himself that he doesn't want her to come back at all. He wants her to run and keep running, as fast and far as she can.

As you can see, voice is intimately tied to how characters feel and express their emotions through a variety of cues and interactions. The better you get to know your characters or mine your own narrative experience, the more vividly voice comes through.

In Summary

- **Emotional expression shapes character voice:** Some characters express emotions intensely, living out their grief or joy openly. Others suppress or hide their emotions, often resulting in a stoic or controlled demeanor. The emotional depth of a character helps to build a memorable voice.

- **Emotional coping shapes voice:** The way characters cope with stress or difficult emotions shapes their voices and adds depth to their personalities.

- **Physical action cues:** Characters sometimes express emotions physically when they can't or won't speak them. Use body language to reflect their emotions.

- **Embodiment:** The way characters physically inhabit their bodies can reveal their emotional states or struggles, enhancing their unique voices and experiences.

- **Sensory cues:** Using senses like sight, smell, and touch can ground a character's emotions in their physical world and provide deeper insight into their emotional state.

- **Dialogue cues:** The way characters speak—their word choice, tone, and interactions—can directly express their emotions and contribute to their voice.

- **Thought cues:** Internal thoughts provide insight into a character's emotional state, revealing what they might not say aloud or how they process their experiences emotionally.

VOICE LESSONS

Writing Exercises

Now, you give it a try!

Manner of Expression

Freewrite some answers about your character's manner of emotional expression:

1. How does your character or narrator speak? Are they loquacious and long winded? Terse and to the point? Cracking jokes? Using idioms and metaphors?

2. What is their personality like and how does this manifest in their thoughts and dialogue? Are they broody but funny? Caustic and dark? Optimistic and cheerful?

3. What other influences shape their voice? Geographical location, a job or hobby, the influence of other people, culture, family, language, etc.?

Then, write a scene in which the character is interacting with someone they've just met, and use their speech patterns to reveal both personality and influence. Show how these factors blend into their voice through the details of the scene.

Dramatic Emotion

- Begin a letter in your character's or narrator's voice to someone they are angry at, beginning with, "First of all..."

- Your character or narrator has been asked to give a speech at an event because of their passionate stance on a cause. Write it.

- Your character or narrator is recounting to a trusted person something funny, ridiculous, or strange that happened to them.

The Suppressed or Avoided Emotion

- What doesn't your character or narrator want to feel? What are they avoiding or hiding from, or hiding from others?

- Write a scene in which your character or narrator is trying to avoid a feeling but unsuccessful.

Coping Mechanisms

Look at each of the following emotions and think of your character or narrator. Write a couple of lines for as many emotions as you can about how your character handles these emotions and what they do about them.

- **Anger:** Do they explode easily? Stuff anger until they finally burst? Do they rant? Do they think angry invectives they don't say? Do they write in a journal or go to kickboxing class to work it out?

- **Sorrow:** Do they cry openly or withdraw into moody silence? Do they internalize or go to yoga class to move through it? Do they seek counseling?

- **Joy:** Even happy people express their joy differently. Some people are outspoken about their joy, announcing it on their social media, while others might have an air of quiet confidence.

- **Disappointment:** Do they beat themselves up for what they did wrong, or how shitty their luck is? Do they take failure as a sign to "try harder?"

> *"People do not seem to realize that their opinion of the world is also a confession of character."*
>
> —Ralph Waldo Emerson

CHAPTER 4

Voice as Opinion and Judgment

How Opinion and Judgment Shape Voice

We've talked about how voice emerges in part from a character's or narrator's experiences in their childhood and formative years, their culture, family, and time period, plus considerations of race, gender, and personality. Now we move on to see how a character's opinions of people, events, and the world inform voice. Opinions, let us remember, are not always based on fact. They can run the gamut from a strong feeling to anecdotal evidence to something a person believes to be fact but which they haven't confirmed for themselves. Opinions are often rooted in beliefs, values, and personal history.

In this chapter, you'll learn how characters' and narrators' opinions shape voice, reveal deep layers of personality, and drive narrative conflict and growth.

First, let's look at a few different kinds of opinions:

Unsolicited Opinions

Social media abounds with opinions you didn't want and didn't seek out, but which people took it upon themselves to offer, often under the guise of being helpful. Somewhere I read a meme that said, "All unsolicited advice is criticism."

This kind of advice could look like a well-meaning family member at a holiday dinner saying, "Writing is a great hobby, but it's not a stable career" when you didn't ask for their opinion. It could be diet advice when you post about having enjoyed a piece of cake, and many variations therein.

Informed Opinions

From doctors and scientists to people with lived experience that grants them a kind of expertise, informed opinions are those that make a case based on knowledge. For example, let's say a farmer recognizing that climate change is going to require her to change up her farming practices is trying to explain this to another farmer who refuses to accept that truth.

"I've been reading up on how extreme weather patterns have been affecting crops lately. It's pretty clear that climate change is having a real impact—longer droughts, unpredictable rainfall, you name it. I'm seeing it firsthand on my farm," she might say.

"Oh, that's just political noise," the disbeliever might respond.

Argumentative Opinions

This could be an opinion that's trying to make a case for something, from a lawyer in a court of law, to a political debate, to a family member trying to persuade another to make a change. These opinions have an agenda.

The internet abounds with people arguing their POV from behind a screen. Say someone who has recently learned of the ills of too much screen time is talking with a friend who lets their child have unlimited time online says, "Social media is harmful to teenagers! It tanks their mental health, disrupts their self-image, and fills their lives with superficial interactions. You should really cut them off."

Argumentative opinions may also mean well, but also can come across as unwanted advice or put someone on the defensive.

Defensive Opinions

On the other end of an argumentative opinion might be someone forced to offer up their defensive opinion, to protect themselves, explain away behavior, or stop something from happening. That parent with the kid who gets too much screen time might defend their parenting style:

"You try entertaining a grumpy tween at the end of your sixty-hour work week. He spends plenty of time outdoors and with his friends, and I'm too exhausted to fight about this."

Friendly Opinions

Not all differences lead to conflict. Sometimes characters or your narrator can hold different opinions and discuss them in a friendly or generative way. Two people sharing experiences they've had and learning from each other, or even a gentle ribbing about their differing tastes in music, partners, or movies.

Hidden Opinions

Characters often harbor opinions they won't readily express aloud, revealed through subtle body language or internal thought. These can foreshadow future conflicts.

What other kinds of opinions can you think of?

In Chapter 3, we discussed how emotion shapes expression, but emotion also underscores opinion and rings loudly through voice. If we take opinion by the dictionary definition to mean a view or judgment, not necessarily based on or shaped by fact or knowledge, you can see how opinion is potentially loaded with emotional shrapnel. Not all judgments or opinions are negative, however. They

VOICE AS OPINION AND JUDGMENT

can also be an estimation of the quality of something or someone—a form of discernment that can even be tied to intuition.

What this means is that your characters' opinions are as unique, varied, and individual as they are, and it's a great way to demonstrate voice.

In addition to shaping voice, giving your characters / narrators a strong opinion can:

- Reveal character

- Shows their limiting beliefs / character flaws, giving them a trajectory of change

- Explain their actions / behaviors

- Set up conflict / opposition with other characters

- Help deliver information about people, places, and things

Let's look at how opinions play out in literature. Here's another example from Teri Bayus's novel, *The Greatest of Ease*, where her opinion may be masking feelings she's not ready to cope with:

> After the circus, I knew my life would become a dinner-party anecdote. My stories were now presented among matching plates for the pinkies-up crowd. At these parties, the soulless stick-figure crowd would swirl their Riedel wine glasses like they know the dif-

ference between swill and grape juice. Then they'd pick through appetizers of soggy crackers with organic sprouts, pretending to be attentive to the other guests' untruths. My new husband consorted weekly with these humorless leviathans as an act of salesmanship for his political climbing. It was a requirement that I attend, but there were always caveats.

What opinions are coming through in this excerpt? (And though we haven't delved much into tone yet, consider the tone—how it makes you feel, what emotions might be loaded within it.)

Gail is done with the circus, a wild and complicated time in her life which, while it was messy, dangerous, and at times unfulfilling, was also enlivening, exhilarating. A place where a wide cast of people joined together like a family.

Now, back in "real" life, Gail's circus life, which meant so much to her, has become nothing more than "dinner-party anecdotes" for the "pinkies-up crowd." Her opinion of them in this line might just be that they're a little fancy or wealthy, but as we go deeper into the description, her opinion takes a turn toward judgment. She calls it the "soulless stick-figure crowd" and taunts that they hardly know the difference between "swill and grape juice." And their behavior isn't much better, in her estimation. They pretend to be attentive, and by the final line, she's pretty much had it with them, calling them "humorless leviathans."

Emotions run latent beneath these opinions. Gail seems to feel less-than in their very presence, as though her past is cheapened. You could also read her opinion of them as self-protective. Maybe she feels insecure and is getting the jump on judging them before they can judge her, to soften the blow.

Now let's look at an opinion born of privilege but also wariness that comes through in this excerpt from Megan Abbott's crime novel *Beware the Woman*. In it, a pregnant white woman named Jacy, who vacations with her relatively new husband at his father's rural home, experiences a menacing tension whenever she's around his father and finds herself resisting his suggestions.

> I nodded vaguely. It all felt a little haphazard, like the time I had a UTI on spring break and my friends summoned the "hotel doctor," a man in a sherbet-colored sports shirt and Bermuda shorts with a duffel bag of pills and rum on his breath.
>
> Don't be a snob, I told myself. Just because Doctor Craig was a "country doctor"—was that the right phrase?—didn't mean he wasn't a good one. In fact, he was probably better. Better bedside manner even, right?
>
> But what did that matter anyway? And what did it matter if no one had yet asked me if I wanted to come here at all? I was bleeding and that was what mattered. The only thing that mattered.

Like Gail from the circus novel, protagonist Jacy also is passing judgment on someone—in this case, a doctor her husband's father has taken her to after she begins bleeding a little, who feels "less qualified" to her by dint of his status as a "country doctor." While in Gail's case, the judgment feels preemptive, protective, here it comes through with a different energy. They're in a rural area, and she's judging the doctor and comparing him to one she saw in Bermuda "with a duffel bag of pills and rum on his breath," though at the same time chastising herself not to be "a snob." This character seems to know and accept about herself that she's judging him, but there's a tension of knowing that if she wasn't essentially trapped too far from a bigger hospital, she might never have consented to see him.

Finally, let's look at an example of opinion born of desperation from Mona Awad's brilliantly scathing, slightly supernatural novel of chronic pain and Shakespeare, *All's Well*. Protagonist Miranda, a drama teacher at a high school, suffers from unspecified pain that often has her lying on the floor of her office at work, as she is in this excerpt.

> I'm lying on the floor watching, against my will, a bad actress in a drug commercial tell me about her fake pain. "Just because my pain is invisible," she pleads to the camera, "doesn't mean it isn't real." And then she attempts a face of what I presume to be her invisible suffering. Her brow furrows. Her mouth is a thin grimace. Her dim eyes attempt to accuse something vague in the distance, a god perhaps. Her bloodless complexion is convincing, though they probably achieved this with makeup and lighting. You can do a lot with makeup and lighting, I have learned.

She looks imploringly at the camera, at me really, for this is a targeted ad based on all of my web searches, based on my keywords, the ones I typed into Google in the days when I was still diagnosing myself. She looks withered but desperate, pleading. She wants something from me. She is asking me to believe her about her pain.

I don't, of course.

Unlike Gail, whose opinion derives from self-protection, and Jacy, whose opinion is shaped by privilege, Miranda's opinion is shaped by pain. Watching an actress, a "bad" one, no less, fake her pain in a commercial, Miranda's loathing is barely contained. She tears apart the actress with her "thin grimace," her "bloodless complexion," loathing oozing out from her every thought. However, we find her judgments less harsh because we know they're grounded in agony, which softens the tone.

Shaping Opinion

When you think about the opinions of your own characters or narrator and how that extends to voice, consider many of the same elements we looked at in Chapter 1. What sorts of circumstances have shaped their opinions? Maybe they were raised by doctors and prioritize medical science and are likely to have a strong opinion on people's health choices. Maybe they had a traumatic experience and believe everyone should get therapy (or that it's better to suppress and avoid). Maybe they grew up in a religion that shaped their beliefs. Maybe their culture, region, time period, gender, or other factors have influenced their opinion. Maybe, like the character in *All's Well*, chronic pain has shaped their opinion.

Opinion in Thoughts or Narrative Voice

Often, a character's or narrator's opinions can't be spoken aloud, so they come through in internal reflections and thoughts, which reveal that information to the reader in an often "private" way. Here's an example from R.F. Kuang's bestselling novel, *Yellowface*, in which a white author steals the work of her Chinese-American friend, Athena, and passes it off as her own after her friend's untimely passing. The thoughts reveal her true opinion of her supposed friend (more specifically, in the narrative voice, understood to be the character's thoughts).

> I used to think that she was simply aloof. Athena is so stupidly, ridiculously successful that it makes sense she wouldn't want to mingle with mere mortals. Athena, presumably, chats exclusively with blue check holders and fellow bestselling authors who can entertain her with their rarefied observations on modern society. Athena doesn't have time to make friends with proletarians.
>
> But in recent years, I've developed another theory, which is that everyone else finds her as unbearable as I

do. It's hard, after all, to be friends with someone who outshines you at every turn. Probably no one else can stand Athena because they can't stand constantly failing to measure up to her. Probably I'm here because I'm just that pathetic.

Thought is a great realm for loading up opinion that characters can't or won't speak aloud, the realm of "brutal truth" and "shameful secrets."

Opinions in Dialogue

A character who says exactly what they think and feel can also create a powerful voice, especially if it's truth-telling, confrontational, or revealing.

Dialogue is a great way to let a character's opinion come through, especially when it opposes other characters. Here's an example from Bonnie Garmus's novel *Lessons in Chemistry*, about a woman scientist, Elizabeth Zott, in the 1950s, who must fight to be given respect for her brilliance (among other things). Notice her forthright manner of talking in the passage below.

> About three weeks later, Calvin and Elizabeth were walking out to the parking lot, their voices raised.
>
> "Your idea is completely misguided," she said. "You're overlooking the fundamental nature of protein synthesis."
>
> "On the contrary," he said, thinking that no one had

ever called any of his ideas misguided and now that someone had, he didn't particularly like it, "I can't believe how you completely ignore the molecular struc—"

"I'm *not* ignoring—"

"You're forgetting the two covalent—"

"It's *three* covalent bonds—"

"Yes, but only when—"

"Look," she interrupted sharply as they stopped in front of her car. "This is a problem."

"What's a problem?"

"*You*," she said firmly, pointing both hands at him. "You're the problem."

"Because we disagree?"

If this scene were written today, it probably wouldn't stand out much for Elizabeth's directness and willingness to interrupt a man with her more informed opinion; but in the '50s, an opinion of that sort could have gotten her blackballed at her place of work and made it less likely for her to "find a husband" as the edict of the day demanded of women.

Changing Opinions

Not only does opinion reveal voice, but it's also a way you can show a character or narrator's transformation arc over the course of a story. Early opinions that are founded in a lack of knowledge or experience can widen and change over the story. A character who begins in a cynical, scared, or uncertain place may find themselves in a more open, brave, or certain place by the end.

Here are a few examples of novels in which the characters' opinions are radically different by the end of the book:

In *An American Marriage,* a novel by Tayari Jones, married couple Celestial and Roy both undergo significant changes in their views of love, loyalty, and justice after Roy is wrongfully imprisoned for twelve years.

At the start of the novel, for Roy, who is adopted (a secret he keeps from his wife until after they are married and pregnant), starting his own family is a chance to do things differently, to free himself from the unwanted inheritances of his past, of himself ... or so he thinks.

> After a year, I was ready to get this show on the road, creating a new generation with an updated set of rules and regulations.

After he is out of prison, his relationship with Celestial has ended and he's in a new relationship, he realizes that he was only trying to outrun himself, and he has a new attitude.

> But mostly my life is good, only it's a different type of good from what I figured on. Some days I get antsy and start talking to Davina about pulling up stakes and starting over in Houston, New Orleans, or even Portland. She humors me, but when I'm done, she smiles because we both know I'm not going anywhere… This is home. This is where I am.

In the memoir *Educated*, Tara Westover grows up isolated in a survivalist family where she is homeschooled and controlled by her brutal father. Her view of education, family, and her own identity evolves dramatically as she seeks higher education outside the bounds of her family and ultimately pursues her own freedom.

As Westover breaks free from her father's controlling worldview for the first time, she doesn't just go on to have a mind opening experience; she simmers in rage.

> I spent two years enumerating my father's flaws, constantly updating the tally, as if reciting every resentment, every real and imagined act of cruelty, of neglect, would justify my decision to cut him from my life. Once justified, I thought the strangling guilt would release me and I could catch my breath. But vindication has no power over guilt.

While her path isn't straightforward, she gains relief from her emotions, and clarity about life, the further she gets from her family, changing her opinion of her own suffering.

> Everything I had worked for, all my years of study, had been to purchase for myself this one privilege: to see and experience more truths than those given to me by my father, and to use those truths to construct my own mind. I had come to believe that the ability to evaluate many ideas, many histories, many points of view, was at the heart of what it means to self-create.

But not entirely. Her opinion has changed, but it's shaped by the trauma she endured.

> I shed my guilt when I accepted my decision on its own terms, without endlessly prosecuting old grievances, without weighing his sins against mine. Without thinking of my father at all. I learned to accept my decision for my own sake, because of me, not because of him. Because I needed it, not because he deserved it.

In the literary novel *Normal People,* by Sally Rooney, protagonists Connell and Marianne are vastly different people. Connell is popular and well-liked but inhabits a false persona. Marianne is odd and unpopular, but truer to herself. They both change significantly in terms of how they view themselves and each other over the course of the novel. Connell gets in closer touch with his authenticity and Marianne comes out of her shell, but in doing so, their relationship with each other also changes.

Early on, Marianne's traumatic experiences at home have left her feeling different from other teens her age. She doesn't like herself, and doesn't understand them:

> Marianne's classmates all seem to like school so much and find it normal. To dress in the same uniform every day, to comply at all times with arbitrary rules, to be scrutinised and monitored for misbehavior, this is normal to them. They have no sense of the school as an oppressive environment.

Much later in the novel, Marianne's opinion of herself and others changes when she has had enough loving experiences (many with Connell) to heal her of this attitude:

> Marianne is neither admired nor reviled anymore. People have forgotten about her. She's a normal person now.

Character and narrator opinions play an essential part in creating voice. As we've seen through a variety of examples, the spectrum of opinion—from unsolicited to hidden, informed to defensive—helps you reveal the complexities that live within your characters.

As you play with opinion to shape voice, consider what unspoken judgments your characters harbor, or how their biases might shift over the course of your story. Allowing your characters' opinions to evolve is not only a hallmark of compelling fiction; it's a reflection of our own changing perspectives.

In Summary

- **Voice reflects opinion:** A character's or narrator's opinions, whether solicited or not, shape their voice, revealing their personality, values, and worldview.

- **Types of opinions:** Different types of opinions include unsolicited opinions (like advice), informed opinions (based on knowledge or experience), argumentative opinions (designed to persuade), defensive opinions (to protect oneself), and friendly exchanges (where characters respectfully discuss differing views).

- **Emotion and opinion:** Opinions are often driven by emotions, and these judgments—whether harsh or empathetic—become an integral part of a character's voice.

- **Opinions reveal character:** A character's opinions can expose their flaws, biases, or limiting beliefs and set the stage for character growth and conflict. Strong opinions often trigger change or development.

- **Internal reflection and narrative voice:** Characters' / narrators' internal thoughts and reflections are powerful tools for revealing their opinions, particularly when they can't voice them aloud. These can expose raw truths, biases, and insecurities.

- **Opinion in dialogue:** Dialogue is a great tool for expressing opinions, particularly when they conflict with others.

- **Shifting opinions:** Over the course of a story, a character's opinion may evolve, reflecting their growth, new experiences, or changing circumstances. This transformation deepens character arcs and adds complexity to their voice.

VOICE LESSONS

Writing Exercises

Now, you give it a try!

Opinion in Opposition

Imagine a situation in which your character has a strong opinion on a subject (politics, religion, family, career choices, etc.), but someone they care about has a conflicting view. Write a scene in which your character passionately expresses their opinion in opposition to the other person's. Stay true to their voice, using their language, background, and emotional state to shape their argument. Think about how their tone might shift based on the relationship with the person they're debating with. Is it more respectful, condescending, defensive, or aggressive? Use dialogue and inner thoughts to convey the character's internal conflict, if any.

PROMPT:

- "I don't think you understand what's at stake here."

- "You have no idea what you're talking about."

Opinion in Dialogue

Write a conversation between two characters during which they each express different opinions on the same topic. Make sure each character's opinion feels authentic to who they are, using dialogue to highlight contrasts in their beliefs and values. Pay attention to how the characters might interrupt or talk over each other.

PROMPT:

- "I've been telling you for years, but you never listen!"
- "You think I'm wrong, but you can't prove it."

Write a Rebuttal Letter

Your character has just received a letter, text, or email from someone expressing an opinion that they strongly disagree with. They are going to write a rebuttal. Have your character outline a logical, emotional, or moral argument in defense of their beliefs, staying true to their voice. The tone might vary depending on the character—some might be formal, others might be more emotional or sarcastic. Focus on how the character might try to convince the other person, or perhaps even dismiss them outright.

PROMPT:

- "I can't believe you think that about me."
- "I'm not going to let this slide."

Thinking Things They Can't Say Aloud

Write a scene where your character is witnessing an event—maybe a family gathering, a political debate, or an emotional confrontation—but they're unable to express their thoughts. Focus on the character's internal monologue, showing their opinion on the situation, even if they can't voice it out loud. How do they feel about the way others are acting? How do they react inwardly to comments they disagree with, or situations that challenge their beliefs?

PROMPT:

- "They have no idea what they're talking about."
- "Why does it always come back to this?"

"Writing is a bit like being a god."

—Charlie Higson

CHAPTER 5

Narrative Voice Vs. Character Voice (A Nod to POV)

Point of View and Voice

You'll often hear phrases tossed around like "narrative voice" or "authorial voice" and it can be confusing as to how this voice is different from your characters' voices, or *if* they are different at all.

For a shorthand, let's consider narrative voice like a current that carries and contains *all* the voice in the novel or memoir. Voice is the water and the waves, but it's also the seaweed, the seahorse, the shark, the sand. The characters are, then, as I write in my book *Writing the Intimate Character*, "like the swimmer stroking through it."

The narrative voice is there to hold the interstices of story together, to relay information that might not come directly through the characters' "words and deeds," and to generally be the story glue that communicates necessary information.

To explain this type of voice more fully, we briefly need to talk about point of view (POV) and its relationship to character voice. For the memoirists and essayists, hang tight, or hang tight until Chapter 6, where I talk about narrative voice in the context of *your* work, though more and more nonfiction writers are turning to the tools of fiction.

Locus of Perception

Point of view is all about the "locus of perception"—in other words, the distance and position from which you convey the source of a character's thoughts, feelings, beliefs, and sensations to the reader. To really understand if you're using the omniscient versus an intimate third person, think of POV as being either internal or external. When you're internal to your protagonist, the reader has access to *only* their thoughts, feelings, perceptions, and spoken dialogue. A way to verify this is to look for perceptual words. When you're external, you can offer info from any other locus (though you need to do it carefully).

Perceptual Words

It also helps to understand what perceptual words are, which cue the reader that you've jumped into someone's POV. Here are examples of different kinds of perceptual words (also known as "filter" words, which we'll talk about in the section on mechanics).

- **Sensory:** Saw, tasted, smelled, felt, heard, sensed, etc.

- **Intellectual:** Knew, understood, perceived, learned, wondered, decided, considered, etc.

- **Emotional:** Yearned, wanted, dreamed, loved, ached, enjoyed, etc.

Now let's look at the main points of view and how they shape voice differently.

Omniscient POV

I like to think of omniscient voice as an all-knowing librarian who has access to every bit of knowledge under the sun—past, present, and future—and who can communicate it without always needing the characters to impart this to the reader. Omniscience used to be the style of the day until about 1900, but its usage has sparingly lingered into contemporary times for a variety of reasons. In an increasingly "me-centric" culture (hello, influencer era), sometimes it feels like we're slowly being conditioned away from it toward first-person narrators, however, it still crops up and it has a powerfully unique effect on voice when done well.

For one, the omniscient narrator can reveal information that the main characters might not know—like what the villain is up to; what other characters are doing in another location; information that falls in the past or future, outside of the front story; details about a place, a plot, even people's personalities or history as well as intimately inside the character's head. This means it can also feel like a wholly separate or overarching voice to that of the characters within the story.

Sometimes, a story reads like omniscience but is actually one character telling another character's story, essentially spilling the tea on someone else's life. In that case, it feels like omniscience, but isn't.

Omniscience can act like a magic camera that can be as up close and intimate (inside a character's head) or as distant as you need (an eagle looking down from the sky). This POV can pull back and offer judgments about the characters that they may or may not think about themselves, then drift closer, internal to their experience. Sometimes, this puts the reader as more of a witness to the story than a participant in it.

Here's an example from Maggie O'Farrell's novel *Hamnet*.

> Every life has its kernel, its hub, its epicentre from which everything flows out, to which everything returns. This moment is the absent mother's: the boy, the empty house, the deserted yard, the unheard cry. Him standing here, at the back of the house, calling for the people who had fed him, swaddled him, rocked him

NARRATIVE VOICE VS. CHARACTER VOICE (A NOD TO POV)

to sleep, held his hand as he took his first steps, taught him to use a spoon...

The locus of perception is *external*, offering information *about* the character, not from within. It has an almost calm, dispassionate tone, disconnected from how the events it describes affect the characters; it is like the substrate, holding together all the disparate bits in between character expression.

Now notice how O'Farrell draws the locus of perception intimate, internal, to the character of Hamnet in a different excerpt:

> He is just about to slide out the drawer where the twists of thread are kept, and the boxes of buttons—carefully, carefully, because he knows the drawer will squeak—when a noise, a slight shifting or scraping, reaches his ears.

How do we know we're in Hamnet's POV versus the narrative voice? There's a character present in the excerpt identified as "he" (Hamnet), and the perceptual words cue us, like "he knows" and "reaches his ears." These words reveal the source of this information (locus of perception) is within the boy himself. The omniscient voice can move in and out of characters' minds, which allows it to shift in tone or proximity, sometimes differing from how a character's voice might sound directly.

While omniscient POV can be difficult to master, what's wonderful about it is that it can allow for a very voicey story, as well as a multitude of voices, to pass judgment on your own characters within the voice of the story, and to set the tone for your story. Recently, my friend, author Steven Dunn, visited my writing class and described the process of collaborating on the novel *Tannery Bay* with his co-author, Katie Jean Shinkle. He said it took them a while to find the unified narrative voice of their novel, while they could each inhabit some of the characters' voices a little more individually.

That narrative voice is one of the things I love about the novel, and they've also used the device that every chapter begins with the words, "Once upon a time ..."

> Once upon a time on Bowfin Street, across the bridge from the dilapidated casino, everybody wakes up all at once from the same dream.

Or:

> Once upon a time on Bowfin Street, the sky holds a pink hue unlike anything anyone in Tannery Bay has ever seen, an iridescent film like the top of the bay. People all over the neighborhood stop walking and drinking coffee and flipping Open signs on storefronts and talking to each other to look to the sky.

Though mastering omniscience can be difficult from a story and structure standpoint, I love how Dunn and Shinkle use it in their novel to evoke a dreamlike voice, a sense of the surreal that is both eerie and beautiful.

NARRATIVE VOICE VS. CHARACTER VOICE (A NOD TO POV)

One more example of omniscience comes from Donna Tartt's novel, *The Little Friend*, a sprawling novel that straddles the literary and mystery genres.

> Harriet had none of her sister's dreamy fragility. She was sturdily built, like a small badger, with round cheeks, a sharp nose, black hair bobbed short, a thin, determined little mouth. She spoke briskly, in a reedy, high-pitched voice that for a Mississippi child was oddly clipped, so that strangers often asked where on earth she had picked up that Yankee accent. Her gaze was pale, penetrating, and not unlike Edie's. The resemblance between her and her grandmother was pointed, and did not go unremarked; but the grandmother's quick, fierce-eyed beauty was in the grandchild merely fierce, and a trifle unsettling.

We know it's omniscient because Harriet herself would be unlikely to think of herself in any of these terms, no matter how precocious a child she is. The omniscient voice here feels a little more acerbic, judgmental, a sharp observing eye that doesn't have time for pleasantries or dreams. It is neither as dispassionate as the one in *Hamnet*, which seems to be almost just reporting the facts, nor as dreamlike as the one in *Tannery Bay*.

Omniscient Roving Heads

Another kind of omniscience its worth mentioning here, which I like to call omniscient roving heads, because it might have you hewing closer to character voice while maintaining the power to move between POVs. It manifests in Celeste Ng's novel, *Little Fires Everywhere,* in which the POV moves between multiple characters' minds in a single scene, shifting the locus of perception to follow the action.

In the following scene, the characters are discussing an adopted baby girl named Mirabelle, whose Chinese birth mother has recently decided she regrets giving her up for adoption (which was done out of desperation and poverty). We're at the house of the Richardsons, a wealthy white family where Mirabelle's adoptive mother, Mrs. McCullough, is visiting with the baby. Trip and Moody are the Richardson sons, and Izzy is the daughter. Pearl is their friend, a girl whom both boys are interested in. I've bolded the places where the perceptual cues tell us whose POV we're in.

> "But she must have had a name before," Izzy said. "Don't you know what it is?"
>
> As a matter of fact, **Mrs. McCullough did know**. The baby had been tucked in a cardboard box, wearing several sets of clothing and cocooned in blankets against the January cold. There had been a note in the box, too...*This baby name May Ling. Please take this baby and give her a better life...*
>
> "I do *not* get the obsession," Moody murmured to Trip, in the corner behind the kitchen island, where they

had retreated with paper plates of quiche and pastries. "They eat. They sleep. They poop. They cry. I'd rather have a dog."

"But girls love them," said Trip. "I bet if Pearl were here she'd be all over that baby."

Moody could not tell whether Trip was mocking him or simply thinking about Pearl himself. He wasn't sure which possibility **bothered** him more.

So, whose two POVs do we get in this passage? First, we have Mrs. McCullough: "As a matter of fact, Mrs. McCullough did know." We have a perceptual word there: *know*.

But a few paragraphs later, in the same scene, we have: "Moody could not tell" and "He wasn't sure which," both perceptual phrases that tell us we are now inside Moody's mind.

The narrative voice often has a different tone or feeling from the character's voice. It might seem dispassionate, impartial, lyrical, forceful, serious, even humorous, while your characters may be anything but. This tends to work best in some form of omniscience because when you're in an intimate, internal POV like first person or third-person intimate, the reader expects that the voice in every line, in some way or another, belongs to the protagonist.

Third-Person Intimate

Let's move on to what some people call "close third" or "deep third person," and which I call "third-person intimate." This POV is one of the most versatile of them all, and probably the most common. It offers almost as much intimacy as first person, but with some distance. Though you use he / she / they pronouns, the reader still feels very close to the character, much like first person, and the information revealed is "internal" to the character.

Here's an example from Anjali Enjeti's novel *The Parted Earth*:

> A pair of Papa-ji's reading spectacles sat on the bedside table. Deepa could reason with him. She could do this tonight, when he returned from work, after her mother had gone to bed. She would convince him they should leave Delhi. She knew she could find a way to make him understand.
>
> She rose, kissed her mother on the cheek. "I'm going to go finish my assignments, Mummy-ji. You rest."

Notice how you could change out the pronouns from he / she to "I" and you would hardly have to change a thing, nor would the intimacy change much.

In third-person intimate, you're still inside your character's experience despite the he / she / they pronouns. There shouldn't be external descriptions of your character unless they're conveyed through another character's eyes, a mirror, or in dialogue.

Your character will not be able to observe her own "rosy cheeks" or "sardonic smile."

However, you could write that she "felt the heat of embarrassment burning her face," or "the muscles in her cheeks strained to hold this false smile of cheer."

Third-person intimate allows you to really hone your characters' voices without having to also consider the narrative voice. There is only character voice.

First-Person POV

First-person POV is one of the most intimate you can find (I'd argue that only a variation of second person, where the character is essentially talking to themselves, is the most intimate). Using "I" pronouns, it puts the reader directly inside the characters' heads. Memoirists and essayists also tend to rely upon the first-person POV, though some writers experiment).

Let's look at an excerpt from David Mitchell's genre-bending novel (though I'd say it leans toward the sci-fi), *Cloud Atlas*:

> I fling open my bedroom curtains, and there's the thirsty sky and the wide river full of ships and boats and stuff, but I'm already thinking of Vinny's chocolaty eyes, shampoo down Vinny's back, beads of sweat on Vinny's shoulders, and Vinny's sly laugh, and by now my heart's going mental and, God, I wish I was

waking up at Vinny's place in Peacock Street and not in my own stupid bedroom. Last night, the words just said themselves, "Christ, I really love you, Vin," and Vinny puffed out a cloud of smoke and did this Prince Charles voice, "One must say, one's frightfully partial to spending time with you, too, Holly Sykes," and I nearly weed myself laughing, though I was a bit narked he didn't say "I love you too" back.

I adore first-person voices because they are so entrenched inside character that it feels like voice personified. It's hard *not* to enter voice in first person, because you're so deeply inside a character's head. In Mitchell's example, this character, Holly, is a teenager so desperately in love with Vinny that she can hardly see straight, and her passion and obsession come through not only in word choice but sentence structure—as the entire paragraph is only two distinct sentences.

Holly uses a lot of specific imagery that contributes to her voice, like "thirsty sky" and "chocolaty eyes" and her heart "going mental." Another character might say the sky is pouring rain, or heavy with rain, and that Vinny's eyes are dark brown. Holly's voice emerges from character-driven word choices infused with her personality, brought to us with the help of first person.

Narrative Voice

Now that we've looked at some examples of what the different voices sound like in different POVs, how they create intimacy (or not), and whether they put the reader internal or external to your characters, let's finally discuss narrative voice, and how it differs (and sometimes doesn't) from your characters' / narrator's voices.

Narrative voice gets a little confusing because it sounds as though it is the same thing as omniscient, but *every* POV has a narrative voice.

We need to look at a couple of more examples to really drive the point home. Here's one from Lydia Netzer's novel *How to Tell Toledo from the Night Sky*.

> Irene kept her face steady, her eyes open, pointed at the machine. If she worked until her face melted into the detector, if her brain fell down into the path of the accelerator, if it was penetrated by pions and if a small black hole was created in her skull, then at least she would have finished all the data for this set. She blinked her eyes to wake herself up, clicked the knob, and peered into the machine, like every time before.

In this passage, we gain information about what Irene thinks, though Irene is not telling us directly in "I" pronouns nor are there any perceptual cues through language like "she thought" or "she saw." Yet we understand the information revealed to us to be Irene's perceptions. Sometimes, putting everything into character words and deeds (dialogue and actions) can take more time and be less necessary than just entering the narrative voice. In essence, the narrative voice attempts to offer as seamless a description of events and feelings as possible in a scene to keep the reader's attention. It is "of" the character's point of view, but not "in" it.

To clarify how narrative voice is not only for omniscience, let's look at it inside a first-person POV story.

Another little excerpt is from Matt Haig's novel *The Life Impossible*, in which a retired math teacher with a tragic past, Grace Winters, inherits a run-down house on a Mediterranean island from a long-lost friend and opens herself to mysteries and adventure she could never have imagined. Here, Grace is following instructions left to her in a letter by the friend, to find a man who will take her out to the ocean for a trip that will literally change the course of Grace's life.

> Anxiety made my whole body alert, like the early onset of a panic attack. It was a feeling I was used to. A feeling like my existence was a delicate thread that could vanish in a sudden wind.
>
> My skin prickled.
>
> I knocked. I listened. I heard nothing but cicadas. This would have been a great time to turn around and walk back to my car and forget all about it. Who did I think I was? Harrison Ford? It was ridiculous. But I was sure I could hear something now. Something above the buzz of insects.

So I pushed the door open.

Grace is both character *and* narrator for us in this story. Because it is first-person POV, every bit of information we get comes directly through her experience. Though we may "hear" and "see" other characters, we cannot ever know what they think or feel unless they express it aloud or demonstrate it in some obvious behavior. The narrative voice sometimes is just relaying information about what is happening: "I knocked. I listened. I heard nothing but cicadas." But it's also giving us a taste of her thoughts, steeped in her personality, which are delightfully voicey: "Who did I think I was? Harrison Ford?"

Point of view contributes to voice through the intimacy you achieve and how closely it allows us to enter your characters' experiences. Experimenting thoughtfully with voice allows you to convey emotional truths, sharpen story tension, and craft immersive worlds that resonate deeply with readers. Voice isn't just about style and flourish, after all; it's connecting with characters. Consider whether you have a favorite POV you perhaps are too afraid to stray from. Play with writing in a POV that pushes you out of your comfort zone to see if it opens up anything for your story or voice.

In Summary:

To make things simpler, I've created a handy POV comparison chart in lieu of a typical summary:

POV	Pronouns	Locus of Perception	Intimacy Level	Narrative Voice	Character Voice	Example Use
Omniscient	He / She / They	External and internal; moves freely between characters	Low to high; flexible	Distinct, overarching, can judge or comment on characters / events	Multiple characters, varied tones	Epic novels, complex stories, historical fiction
Omniscient Roving Heads	He / She / They	Shifts between characters within a single scene	Medium to high	Flexible, follows the action closely	Clearly defined per character, shifts frequently	Complex character dynamics, community-based novels
Third-Person Intimate	He / She / They	Internal, limited to one character per scene or section	High; very close to character's internal world	Subsumed entirely within character voice; minimal or no distinct narrative voice	Singular, consistent, deeply personal	Character-driven fiction, contemporary novels
First-Person	I	Internal; deeply personal	Very high; maximum intimacy	Completely integrated into character voice	Singular, deeply intimate, personalized	Memoir, personal essays, intense character-driven novels
Narrative Voice	Depends on POV	Can be external or internal, acts as the connective tissue	Varies; supports chosen POV	Holds together scenes, offers seamless info beyond direct actions / dialogue	Varies based on POV chosen; integrates or supports characters' perspectives	Essential for clarity and cohesion, present in all POVs

VOICE LESSONS

Writing Exercises

Now, you give it a try!

POV Shifting Practice

Take a scene from your current work in progress or write a new one. Begin in one point of view, either omniscient, third-person intimate, or first person, then shift to another. For example, start with a third-person omniscient narration, then move to a character's close third-person perspective. Afterward, reflect on how the change affects the tone, intimacy, and what the reader is able to perceive. Pay special attention to how the different POVs shape voice and how much access you have to characters' inner thoughts and feelings.

Perceptual Word Identification

Write a brief scene from a character's or your narrator's perspective. Focus on using perceptual words like "felt," "saw," "heard," and "understood" to signal where the reader is getting information from the character. Then, go back and highlight all the perceptual words you've used. Reflect on how those words shape the reader's experience and how much access they provide to the character's inner world. Finally, rewrite the scene without any perceptual words—how does the tone and level of intimacy change?

Omniscient Roving Heads

Write a scene with multiple characters in which you shift the point of view between them as the action unfolds. Try to make the transitions between characters' perceptions smooth, using perceptual words and cues that clearly signal whose mind we are in. Can you maintain the different qualities of each character's voice as you shift? Afterward, read through the scene and assess how the shifting POV impacts the flow and tone of the narrative.

> *"A fiction writer starts with meaning and then manufactures events to represent it; a memoirist starts with events, then derives meaning from them."*
>
> —Don DeLillo

CHAPTER 6

When the Character Is You (Memoir + Essay)

Voice in Memoir and Essay

Though we've looked at voice examples in memoirs along the way so far, I want to delve into some memoir-specific elements around voice and tone by talking about who, exactly, is narrating a memoir or essay.

Where the gray area comes in, which also offers stylistic room for memoir and essay writers, is that you are *both* the narrator telling the story—the voice guiding the reader through scenes, reflections, and takeaways—*and* a character in the story, often the protagonist.

This makes you an unreliable narrator *and* an immaculate curator of your own experience—the reader must take for granted that what you tell us is true, but also, truth is malleable, and many times a writer undertakes a memoir or essay to tell *their version* of the truth. One of my favorite examples of this is when writer Lucy Grealy, author of the memoir *Autobiography of a Face*, was asked in an interview about how she remembered everything in her story in order to write it. "I didn't remember it," Grealy said. "I wrote it. I'm a writer."

This doesn't mean you're lying or making up experiences—it means you are arranging the facts, presenting them, and revealing only the parts of yourself and your experiences that you wish to. You are the architect of your story.

Or, as author Carmen Maria Machado says, equally eloquently, in her experimental memoir *In the Dream House*, "The memoir is, at its core, an act of resurrection. Memoirists re-create the past, reconstruct dialogue. They summon meaning from events that have long been dormant. They braid the clays of memory and essay and fact and perception together, smash them into a ball, roll them flat. They manipulate time; resuscitate the dead. They put themselves, and others, into necessary context."

Controlling the Narrative

With the understanding that you are both the character and the narrator, let's examine one of my favorite examples of a memoir that takes full control of how the reader experiences its narrator and shapes voice: Gina Frangello's *Blow Your House Down: A Story of Family, Feminism and Treason*. This memoir delves into the events leading to the affair that ultimately shattered her life. Yet it also tells a story of transformation, one that allowed her to live more authentically despite facing profound challenges, including the death of a best friend, the loss of her beloved mother, and a breast cancer diagnosis, to name a few.

Frangello knows the world has a double standard for women who cheat on their spouses; while men are often allowed to engage in all kinds of awful, sexist, and even abusive behavior and still be seen as upstanding, women are scorned, shunned, and harmed for doing the same.

The opening of the memoir is a chapter called "The Story of A," and in it, Frangello offers a series of stylistic vignettes that tell us what A stands for, like so:

A is for Adulteress

> But you knew that. There is virtually no history of literature without the Adulteress. Anna Karenina, Emma Bovary, Edna Pontelier, Hester Prynne, Daisy Buchanan, Molly Bloom. The adulteress throws herself in front of a train, runs over her husband's lover with a car, walks into the ocean intent on dying without a care for her children. A is for Adulteress, Agent of Ruin. Woman.

Subsequent vignettes include "A" being equivalent to: accused, author, asshole, ancient, antiheroine, and more, and each one tells us a little more about something related to the narrator and / or the overarching worldview of women in these contexts. What Frangello is doing is getting ahead of all our judgments and biases, because if you go into reading the book already having decided her character, you're unlikely to hold an open mind.

But also notice how the voice changes when Frangello drops into the actual lived-experience portions of the memoir. She gives us practical scenes paired with philosophical passages:

> "Don't cry for me when I'm gone," my father recently told my mother. "I'm ready."
>
> My mother relays this to me at my upstairs apartment. She and my father have lived downstairs since my husband and I bought this house in 1999, but my father no longer comes to visit because he can't manage the stairs."

And:

> How do we measure a life's worth? In laughter? In orgasms? In money? In how often we have been photographed? In children borne or raised? In the number of continents on which we have made love? In number of books published? In latest versions of iPads and iPhones? In jazz albums filling a giant trunk in the basement? In years?

I love the voice and tone shifts in her memoir because they reflect many different facets of the author herself.

Some memoirs may not even center the narrator directly, or only indirectly, in contrast or connection to some other key player in their life story. An incredible example of this comes from the memoir *Daughter of the Queen of Sheba* by former NPR radio foreign correspondent, Jacki Lyden. The memoir is about growing up with a mother who suffered extreme mental illness. Her mother is a larger-than-life character who gets a lot of screen time on the page as follows:

> "I am the Queen of Sheba," my mother announced to me in a regal voice. She had taken the silky yellow sheets from her voluptuous bed and twisted them around and around her torso like a toga, leaving one shoulder, as white as a gardenia, bare except for her bra strap...
>
> "I am the Queen of Sheba," she murmured confidentially, "and I bequeath to each of my three daughters a country. To you, Jacki, the oldest Mesopotamia."
>
> ...
>
> I was alone in the house with her, but she might have been on another continent. I could not follow her.

When Lyden tells us about herself, it is almost always in connection to her mother. Lyden, who had an incredible career as a foreign correspondent in war zones, could easily have told another story, but this version of herself—the daughter shaped by her unconventional and often undertreated mother, is the one she chose to share.

Sharing a Part of the Whole

While memoir used to be synonymous with telling one's whole life story, it has now expanded, or perhaps condensed, to allow for *parts* of a story, moments in time, seminal events and experiences. One example of this is award-winning journalist and author Ta-Nehisi Coates's book *Between the World and Me*. It isn't quite a memoir, per se, though it is very much drawn from Coates's own experiences. It is epistolary, written as a letter to his son attempting to address some key questions and concerns about being Black in the United States. Thus, the voice is conversational, a version of Coates that he might not normally share in book form, one in which the reader almost feels like an eavesdropper on a conversation we shouldn't be hearing because it is so personal between father and son.

> Content note: Acts of violence against Black people

> I write you in your fifteenth year. I am writing you because this was the year you saw Eric Garner choked to death for selling cigarettes: because you know now that Renisha McBride was shot for seeking help, that John Crawford was shot down for browsing in a department store. And you have seen men in uniform drive by and murder Tamir Rice, a twelve-year-old child whom they were oath-bound to protect ...
>
> It does not matter if the destruction is the result of an unfortunate overreaction. It does not matter if it origi-

nates in misunderstanding. It does not matter if the destruction springs from a foolish policy...The destroyers will rarely be held accountable.

I'm sure there's vastly more to this father / son story that involves joy and good times as well as the microaggressions and ravages of racism, but the piece that Coates shares in this book is a slice of experience meant to both speak deeply to his son and inform the onlooking reader about realities they might not even be aware of.

Playing with POV in Memoir

Though POV in memoir or essay seems straightforward because it's coming only from one POV, the "I," there's quite a bit of leeway and room for play.

Let's go back to the incredible Carmen Maria Machado's *In the Dream House*, one of the most stunning memoirs I've read in years. It's constructed on the premise that each chapter is a room in a house—the house being a metaphor for her life, her mind, and her experiences.

> **Dream House as Inciting Incident**
>
> You meet her on a weeknight, at dinner with a mutual friend in a diner in Iowa City where the walls are windows. She is sweaty, having just come from the gym, her white-blonde hair pulled back in a short ponytail. She has a dazzling smile, a raspy voice that sounds like a wheelbarrow being dragged over stones. She is that mix of butch and femme that drives you crazy.

> You and your friend are talking about television when she arrives; you have been complaining about men's stories, men's stories, how everything is men's stories. She laughs, agrees. She tells you she's freshly transplanted from New York, drawing unemployment insurance and applying to MFA programs. She's a writer too.
>
> Every time she speaks, you feel something inside you drop. You will remember so little about the dinner except that, at the end of it, you want to prolong the evening and so you order tea of all things. You drink it—a mouthful of heat and herb, scorching the roof of your mouth—while trying not to stare at her, trying to be charming and nonchalant while desire gathers in your limbs. Your female crushes were always floating past you, out of reach, but she touches your arm and looks directly at you and you feel like a child buying something with her own money for the first time.

Each chapter is a vignette with its own little title, and more unique yet, she's writing in the second person, as though she is talking directly to her past selves rather than to an audience of readers. It creates a hyper-intimacy, among other things.

Two Narrative Voices in Memoir and Essay

We've established that the writer and the protagonist are often one and the same in memoir and essay, but the voices with which you present your story may change based on your vantage in time, necessitating two narrative voices.

One voice contains the "you" of the past, or, as Sue William Silverman, author of *Fearless Confessions*, calls it, the "voice of innocence" who lived through your story events. (Innocence doesn't mean you were young and unknowing; it's only a word to contrast with the second voice, or as I like to call it the "voice of the lived moment.") The other voice you will often interweave is the contrasting "voice of experience," as referenced in Brooke Warner's and Linda Joy Myers's book, *Breaking Ground On Your Memoir: Craft, Inspiration and Motivation for Memoir Writers*. The voice of experience is the "you" of today (or at the time of the writing), the meaning maker who processes or analyzes experiences and recounts them to the reader, reflecting on what the voice of innocence went through.

Most essays or memoirs engage in a kind of dialogue or dance between these two voices. Some memoirs, like the bestselling *The Glass Castle* by Jeannette Walls, spend a good portion of their time in the voice of innocence, reading almost like a novel, while others weave in and out of sharing experience as well as analyzing experience.

Voice of Innocence

The voice of innocence can sometimes be the hardest voice to enter for nonfiction writers as it often requires reentering memories, experiences, and moments from your life that are far behind you or that might be emotionally fraught. The voice of innocence is often caught up in the moment of their experience and does not bring the framework of your older or wiser knowledge to bear.

Here is an example from Mireya S. Vela's memoir *Vestiges of Courage*, which details some of the experiences of being raised "between two cultures and two languages."

> The well was fathomlessly deep. Uncovered, I was unable to see the bottom. Grandmother had thrown a bucket in. I had leaned forward as far as my courage allowed and caught the cold smells of the well. The bucket had splashed with an echo.

Notice the immediacy and childlike tone of this voice—how it is right in the moment of an experience and not bringing much else in the way of thoughts to bear.

But not all voice of innocence refers to childhood; it just means in the moment of lived experience, before you started to analyze and make meaning of your experience. Here's another example from Paul Kalanithi's memoir, *When Breath Becomes Air* (whose subject will become obvious as you read the passage):

> I flipped through the CT scan images, the diagnosis obvious: the lungs were matted with innumerable tumors, the spine deformed, a full lobe of the liver obliterated. Cancer, widely disseminated. I was a neurosurgical resident entering my final year of training. Over the last six years, I'd examined scores of such scans, on the off chance that some procedure might benefit the patient. But this scan was different: it was my own.

Here we are "in the moment" of the day an oncology neurosurgical resident grapples with the fact that he has become the patient.

And one more, from Melissa Febos's memoir-in-essays, *Abandon Me*, in which the narrator is a young adult:

> *What about this one?* she asks, lifting my arm and brushing the inside of my wrist with her fingertips.
>
> *My little brother's nickname.*
>
> *And this?* she touches the anatomical heart on my forearm and smiles. *Heart on your sleeve?*
>
> *I like to remember that it's a muscle*, I say.
>
> Her hand slides over the crook of my elbow and grasps my bicep. *This is my favorite*, she says. It is a portrait of Billie Holiday. She is in mid-song. Her features are finely detailed in black. It is my favorite too.
>
> I inevitably guide new lovers through a tour of my tattoos.

The voice of innocence is:

- In the moment (happening in the "now" of the story)
- In scene (setting details, action)
- Sometimes like watching a movie unfolding
- Can include character thoughts and observa-

tions, but these, too, are the kind that accompany events in the moment

Voice of Experience

In contrast to the immediacy and youth of the voice of innocence, often when authors enter the voice of experience, you notice a difference in its cadence and tone, how it holds the wisdom of experience and the tinge of understanding, regret, awareness, or more.

In Mireya S. Vela's memoir, notice how the voice of experience brings a more adult-sounding awareness that the child voice did not have or need to have.

> **Content note: Child abuse**

> I wasn't ready to think then of how my mom was contributing to what was happening to me. One glance. What might it mean if she glanced away as those men cornered me? Would her courage leave her? I wasn't ready to consider how her choices might destroy me. Instead, I chose to believe what she told me, and pretend I didn't think she was lying when she said she loved me.

By bringing in the reflection, we, the readers, are invited to consider, along with Vela, what meaning she is making of her painful past experiences. Vela lays out the generational trauma that allowed parents to pass on pain to their children.

In Febos's example, after being in the moment with her lover describing her tattoos, she enters a voice that analyzes this experience:

> We all want this in love—for our lovers to spot the marks of our losses, the scars that note how we have been changed, how we become the person they love. It's not easy to offer these details. Sometimes, it is impossible. My tattoos make the first move.

And in Kalanithi's memoir, he spends a lot of time alternating between these two voices because he was writing it at the same time as living the experience of his own terminal cancer, unlike many people who are writing a memoir years after having an experience.

> Lying next to Lucy in the hospital bed, both of us crying, the CT scan images still glowing on the computer screen, that identity as a physician—my identity—no longer mattered. With the cancer having invaded multiple organ systems, the diagnosis was clear. The room was quiet. Lucy told me she loved me. "I don't want to die," I said. I told her to remarry, that I couldn't bear the thought of her being alone. I told her we should refinance the mortgage immediately. We started calling family members. At some point, Victoria came by the room, and we discussed the scan and the likely future treatments. When she brought up the logistics of returning to residency, I stopped her.
>
> "Victoria," I said, "I'm never coming back to this hospital as a doctor. Don't you think?"

One chapter of my life seemed to have ended; perhaps the whole book was closing. Instead of being the pastoral figure aiding a life transition, I found myself the sheep, lost and confused.

The voice of experience:

- Is "the meaning maker"

- Is looking back or reflective

- Is wiser than the voice of innocence due to time or experience

- Can add up meaning the narrator did not or could not have at the time

- Fills in information not available to the narrator / reader at the time of the scene

Why bother with this voice of experience? Why not just present everything as it happened? Memoir and essay are often a writer's way of processing an experience to mine it for deeper truth or understanding, particularly painful or challenging ones. If all the reader sees is your pain, but never any more, it might be hard to stay connected to the work. And while I can't say it's universal that everyone reads to seek meaning, I think there's a pretty solid chance that many people are reading memoir for glimmers of truth and connection, to feel less alone, to grieve and laugh along with you.

Body and Mind

If these two voices aren't quite landing yet, another way to conceive of them, as Warner and Myers write, is to think of them as "you the character" as the body, and "you the narrator" as the mind. Thus, "When you are writing as 'you the character' or 'voice of innocence' you should aim to bring the reader physically into the character's experience in scene."

When you write essay or memoir, you alternate between the voice of innocence and the voice of experience. However, some pieces may be written entirely in the voice of innocence, in "the body"—shown in scene and using sensory and embodied details. In crafting your narrator, you want to get to know both "you's."

The body is evident in the voice-of-innocence passages above in one way or another—Febos and her lover are touching arms and wrists, tracing the contours of her tattoos. Kalanithi is looking *inside* his own body, at CT scans that reveal a network of cancer that is changing not just his body, but his identity as a doctor. Vela is drawing upon sensory imagery in the "cold smells" of the well and how "the bucket had splashed with an echo."

Writing both memoir and essay position you as protagonist and storyteller, architect and subject. Through carefully balancing the immediacy of lived experience (the voice of innocence) and the reflective wisdom of hindsight (the voice of experience), you deepen the reader's understanding of your journey.

In Summary

- **The character is you:** In memoir writing, the author is both the narrator guiding the reader and a character in the story, often the protagonist.

- **Curating truth:** Memoirists curate their own experiences, presenting the facts they choose and crafting their narrative in a way that is shaped by memory and perception.

- **Voice of innocence vs. voice of experience:** Memoirists often interweave two voices: the voice of innocence, which is immediate and focused on the experience as it happens, based in bodily and sensory detail; and the voice of experience, which provides reflective, meaning-making commentary on past events.

- **Voice shifts in memoir:** Memoirists can also use changes in voice to reflect the complexity of the author's identity and experiences.

- **Focus beyond the narrator:** Not all memoirs

center on the narrator directly—some may highlight other key "characters" in the narrator's life.

- **Creative memoir formats:** It's possible to use unconventional formats and techniques to create intimate, unique experiences for the reader.

VOICE LESSONS

Writing Exercises

Now, you give it a try!

The Voice of Innocence

Think of a potent memory that carries with it a somewhat strong emotion: an argument you had with a loved one; a time you fell off your bike but no one came to help; a time you fought with a sibling; when you fell in love for the first time...

Try to describe it as though it is happening to you all over again in the moment. You can even write in the present tense (I walk / I say / I do). Try to write in scene: action, dialogue, physical sensations, setting details.

The Voice of Experience

Now, attempt to adopt the "voice of experience" about the same thing you just wrote—the you of today—and tell us about this memory with some sort of observation or reflection. What do you know now that you didn't then? What information can you fill in? What reflections or thoughts do you have now?

Now, write a third paragraph in which you weave in and out of these two voices—perhaps beginning in the voice of innocence, then zooming out in time to offer the analytical voice of experience. Or starting in the voice of experience and dropping backward into a flashback scene.

PART TWO

Mechanisms of Voice

> *"All words are pegs to hang ideas on."*
>
> —Henry Ward Beecher

CHAPTER 7

Syntax and Lexicon

Voice at the Sentence Level

Every writer has a different approach in laying down story and voice. Some people write with the forward thrust of plot or narrative arc, driving the story through character. Others attend to the delicate work of sentences, a detailed and sometimes slow crawl that lays down an intentional track for characters to follow. For a lot of writers, the sentence-level detail is a later one, a place you may return to when you've nailed that story draft.

However, voice and tone in writing rely heavily on the way you organize language—your syntax, or sentence structure, and lexicon, or vocabulary. Yet I chose to leave the mechanics of voice for the second part of this book so the discussion of voice would begin with an *experience* of a variety of voices first, exploring some of the deeper contributions to voice before looking at, in essence, how the sausage is made. While I think the grammar and linguistic elements of voice are fascinating and necessary to understand (though sometimes they might give you a flashback to a grade-school grammar class), they *can* also burden the writing process for some people if you're trying to hold them too much in mind as you write.

That said, these elements will help you make intentional sentence and word-craft choices that undergird and shape voice.

So, here we go!

Syntax: The Architecture of Sentences

"Syntax" is as bureaucratic-sounding a word as "prose" is pretty—it refers to elements with which we structure our sentences (and occasionally, sentence fragments). You can think of it as a set of rules that order language or, perhaps more accurately for this book, the naturally occurring rules of your characters' and narrators' manner of speech that comprise voice (and here, we take speech to refer to all forms of expression: thoughts, dialogue, and narrative voice). If all the elements we've discussed so far comprise voice—the substrate that makes up your character's or narrator's very being—then syntax is the unique architecture of the ways they express those characteristics in speech and thought.

Any syntactical discussions in this book are also made with the understanding that I am a native English speaker and a Gen X, cisgender white woman born and raised in Northern California. I am neither an expert in the syntax and grammar of other languages a writer speaks or was raised around, nor am I suggesting these are the only "correct" rules or that you can't write any damn way you please. I refuse to be the language police; I believe in the fluidity of language and resist institutional ways of keeping people from expressing themselves in ways that are natural to them.

It also needs to be said that there's a lot of classicism and racism embedded in rules of grammar and voice (particularly in North America) that I do not wish to perpetuate in any advice given. So please filter any and all suggestions with your own understanding and knowledge of voice for *your* characters or narrator.

The Author's Syntax

That said, you the writer have a natural syntax you may use without paying much attention to it in your own life. It springs from all the same factors that undergird character and narrator experience, such as where you grew up, how people in your family expressed themselves, your culture, the historical time period you grew up in or are living in, etc. It might also be influenced by things such as physical ability or disability, trauma, religious contexts, your parents' jobs, and much more. The reason fiction writers need to pay attention to *their own* syntax is that it can be difficult to shake it off to give life to *character* syntax. Even essay and memoir writers may find they have to work to curate a voice to tell their story in a way that feels a little different from their "natural" voice. While I don't expect anyone to sentence-diagram their own speech, understand that you may discover some tension in shaping character voices to sound different from your own—and that may require a little effort.

In addition to having a natural syntax, most people also have a lexicon, or vocabulary, of words at their disposal. Imagine this as the grab bag of words familiar to you from which you tend to draw with such ease, you don't even notice it. We don't *only* use these words, but you might use them more frequently and easily than you do others. You might not even be aware of your own lexicon, but I'll bet if you've talked to someone who has a different one, you notice it. You often hear people teased for using "big" words, and you may notice the difference in generational lexicons if you spend a lot of time with people older or younger than you.

Let's start by looking at some different syntax examples to see how they are like those fun molds my son used to squeeze his Play-Doh through, creating shape, texture, and differences from character to character.

Generational Syntax

When talking syntax, I love to start with this example of the main character from Barbara Kingsolver's Pulitzer Prize-winning novel, *Demon Copperhead*, because it is so very voicey. Protagonist Damon (nicknamed Demon) is an Appalachian teen, born to a mother with alcohol struggles and an absent father, who gains a world-weary precociousness through his many traumas.

> My thinking here is to put everything in the order of how it happened, give or take certain intervals of a young man skunked out of his skull box, some dots duly connected. But damn. A kid is a terrible thing to be, in charge of nothing.

Though this character is a young man, the sentence construction for me, beginning with that gerund phrase, "My thinking here," and the way it meanders, feels older, even old-fashioned, like a man who has lived many more years than this character. There's an almost Yoda-like quality of syntax in that final sentence too, with the way she's organized the predicate "a kid is a terrible thing to be" with the prepositional phrase "in charge of nothing." Kingsolver could have just written: "It was terrible to be a kid in charge of nothing" but with this version there's less cadence, rhythm, and voice.

Here's another example that comes from John Green's novel *The Fault in Our Stars*, about a teen diagnosed with cancer. It's worth nothing that this novel was published in 2012, because generational syntax and language changes that quickly. The teens depicted in this passage speak differently than the teens of right now (as the mother of a seventeen-year-old, I have some actionable evidence of this). The ellipsis (…) is mine to speed the passage along.

> The Support Group, of course, was depressing as hell…I noticed this because Patrick, the Support Group Leader and only person over eighteen in the room, talked about the heart of Jesus every freaking meeting, all about how we, as young cancer survivors, were sitting right in Christ's very sacred heart and whatever …
>
> So here's how it went in God's heart: The six or seven or ten of us walked/wheeled in, grazed at a decrepit selection of cookies and lemonade, sat down in the Circle of Trust, and listened to Patrick recount for the thousandth time his depressingly miserable life story—how he had cancer in his balls and they thought he was going to die but he didn't die and now here he is, a full-grown adult in a church basement in the 137th nicest city in America, divorced, addicted to video games, mostly friendless, eking out a meager living by exploiting his cancertastic past, slowly working his way toward a master's degree that will not improve his career prospects, waiting, as we all do, for the sword of Damocles to give him the relief that he escaped lo those many years ago when cancer took both of his nuts but spared what only the most generous soul would call his life. AND YOU TOO MIGHT BE SO LUCKY!

You'll likely notice the extra-long sentence of the second paragraph, which gives it teen-as-golden-retriever energy, or a kind of stream-of-consciousness feeling, as it rushes to its conclusion. It's also an awful lot of time given to something the character proclaims to be depressed or bored by. And much of the vocabulary is designed to feel young (even though, I'd wager, my son's Gen Z cohort would not likely feel this represents how they speak today), with phrasing like "every freaking meeting," and "cancertastic" and the, uh, judgment on their leader's body parts. Moreover, the tone is bored, annoyed, couldn't care less, yet at the same time, a little bit amused, as though the character is entertaining themselves with their own thoughts. It's not to say that a grown adult couldn't write like this, but young is clearly what Green was going for.

That said, as a fifty-something who spends a fair amount of time around Gen Z teens and with Gen Z coworkers in their twenties (and frankly, on social media), I still find myself charmed by the way they express themselves differently from me. For example, a sentence that might come out of my own child's mouth: "I used to think pineapple on pizza was trash, but it's actually kinda fire. You're low-key right."

As a developmental editor, I've noted inaccurate-sounding slang for teens in more than a few adult manuscripts (and I'm not even an expert on modern-day teen slang). It's one of the biggest giveaways, and slang evolves quickly, so be careful of this when working on a time period-based book.

I also love the syntax in an essay titled "English and Spanish" by Myriam Gurba in her collection *Mean*. Myriam comes across as very conversational with short, concise sentences, but she folds in subtle devices, like repetition and parallelism (not to mention, some wonderful dry wit).

> I began as an only child with an only language. This language was English and Spanish.
>
> My English and Spanish came from a pact my parents made. My father, a green-eyed American, agreed to speak to me in English. My mother, a Mexican by birth, a feminist by choice, promised to speak to me in her native Romance language peppered with Nahuatl.
>
> Their pact gave me lots of words. Folger's crystals. Asshole. Aguacata. Tiliche. Cadillac. Smart. Girl. Sanguich. That's Mexican for *sandwich*.

The sentences are short and simple, as though mimicking the child's mind, which takes things at face value. Gurba starts with a delightful little bit of parallelism (using similar grammatical structures to create rhythm or meaning) in "an only child with an only language", which also sets us up for the punchline of the next sentence: "This language was English and Spanish." The reader chuckles, understanding that while those are, in fact, two languages, they are *one* to a child who has been raised with both in her home.

SYNTAX AND LEXICON

Lastly, I want to look at another kind of syntax, from Tess Gunty's award-winning literary novel *The Rabbit Hutch*, which utilizes a kind of poetic syntax (particularly in the second paragraph) for a lyrical effect. Lyrical sentences often ask us to push past your logical, linear, thinking mind and drop more into poetic elements to evoke a particular mood or tone.

> Content note: Describes the results of violence (note that this is the opening of the book, not a spoiler)

On a hot night in Apartment C4, Blandine Watkins exits her body. She is only eighteen years old, but she has spent most of her life wishing for this to happen. The agony is sweet, as the mystics promised. It's like your soul is being stabbed with light, the mystics said, and they were right about that, too.

Knife, cotton, hoof, bleach, pain, fur, bliss—as Blandine exits herself, she is all of it. She is every tenant of her apartment building. She is trash and cherub, a rubber shoe on the seafloor, her father's orange jumpsuit, a brush raking through her mother's hair. The first and last Zorn Automobile factory in Vacca Vale, Indiana. A nucleus inside the man who robbed her body when she was fourteen, a pair of red glasses on the face of her favorite librarian, a radish tugged from a bed of dirt. She is no one. She is Katy the Portuguese water dog, who licked her face whenever the foster family banished them both in the snow because they were in the way. An algorithm for amplified content and a blue slushee from the gas station...

The paragraph goes on for quite a bit longer, infused with metaphors that seem to tell the whole story of her life. Notice that when the syntax itself changes, giving way to a list in the second paragraph—several of which are sentence fragments—the voice changes with it. By the time you hit the words "she is every tenant of her apartment building," "she is trash and cherub..." you're almost singing these words inside your head. They've taken on a hypnotic and wavelike rhythm that is different from the sentences in the first paragraph.

Since the reader is led to believe that Blandine is dying, it makes sense for the syntax to shift from a linear, "conscious mind" process to one that feels less attached to her individual consciousness or identity and thus breaking apart from her typical syntax.

Dialogue Syntax

Additionally, your character's or narrator's syntax might change somewhat between thoughts and dialogue or other methods of communication. This isn't the first time we've discussed that there's often a difference in voice (and tone) of spoken words and internal thoughts. There are many reasons why characters and narrators may modulate their syntax and tone (more to come when we discuss code-switching in Chapter 8) when they speak versus in their thoughts, but it's really only in literature or movies that the reader is privy to that difference in real time by gaining access to both a character's thoughts and dialogue.

Lexicon / Vocabulary

Lexicon is itself a great word, conjuring a magical linguist or mad scientist, as opposed to "vocabulary," which sounds so stodgy. While it might seem impossible to determine the entire scope of words your character or narrator might use, remember that fantasy writer J.R.R. Tolkien (of *Lord of the Rings* fame) created an entire language—Elvish. And famed science fiction writer Ursula K. Le Guin did similarly (*The Left Hand of Darkness*, *The Lathe of Heaven*), because, as she wrote about her process:

"To make up a name of a person or a place is to open the way to the world of languages the name belongs to. It's a gate to Elsewhere. How do they talk in Elsewhere? How do we find out how they talk?"

Science fiction and fantasy writer N.K. Jemisin doesn't start with thinking about the sentences in her breathtaking, high-concept novels; she starts with the flora and fauna of a world before she can create her characters.

In other words, you are more than capable of finding, creating, and opening yourself to words that fit your characters, but it might take thought, brainstorming, and even keeping a lexicon journal.

The Curated Self

For memoirists and essayists, let's come back to the idea of curating. You can think of your writing like a museum display or an interactive piece of performance art, a one-person play. That version of you might sound a little different than your daily self or it might be a side of you that you *choose* to show: your arch side, your lyrical side, or a version of you that is in control.

Let's look at what Gurba does with lexicon in the same essay mentioned above, "English and Spanish," in which she discusses her "only language" which is really an amalgam of her parents' two different languages.

> On my first day, yo hablé con mis nursery school maestras usando palabras como éstas because I assumed we all had the same words. I didn't know I was spewing ciphers fed to me by a foreigner. I didn't know Mexicans *were* Mexicans, a category some mistake for subhuman, a category my grandfather mistakes for the divine.

Her lexicon is built upon the duality of her "two" languages. Yet, to this narrator, they are but one language with a multitude of words to choose from, one that only becomes "unusual" in the eyes of a judging observer.

In another example, Sophie Strand's memoir *The Body Is a Doorway: A Journey Beyond Healing, Hope and the Human*, which explores the ecology and etiology of chronic illness and her love for the natural world, she relies upon language related to nature or science to describe herself and her own experiences:

> I inhaled carefully, imagining the stream as a splint against my spine, correcting me not into straightness, but into its own cursive intelligence. What if my spine was *not* incorrect, but rather liquid, making love with the landscape? The summer sky pressed its blue flesh against my face, sunlight pooling at the bottom of my irises, creating a tidal pool of my eyes: a place for crustaceans and lichen to congregate. Despite my deliberate stillness, my left hip rolled, making a noise like a door unlocking.

Her lexicon is forged from the natural world, and her syntax is often quite lyrical, making lovely poetry out of literary devices (lots of alliteration and metaphor) for experiences that would hit differently in plainer language.

Verbs, Adjectives, and Nouns

Okay, as you move into this next section, you might start to feel like you're back in an English class, but have some faith—what seems "boring" is important, I promise. We're going to talk about parts of speech that you use all the time, and which you might never have thought about as uniquely contributing to voice: Your verbs, adjectives, and nouns.

Verbs

You probably remember that verbs are the muscle and energy of your sentences. The action words that tell you what a character is doing: bounce, kick, sing, run, tell, see, etc. Or as Constance Hale writes in *Sin and Syntax*, "No sentence is complete until you know what the subject did." However, a note here on style: Lots of writers rule-break intentionally to create style and tone, so yes, you can use a sentence fragment, one without a verb, or an unattached dependent clause (a clause with a subject and a verb that is typically dependent on another independent clause) for stylistic or dramatic effect, but it's still helpful to contextualize what verbs are and how to use them.

Where verbs come into voice is that they can serve as reflections of the character's tastes and personality. So, while you *can* use any old functional verb, do they feel true to your character / narrator? Additionally, interesting verbs can add texture and complexity to voice.

Here's an example from a very voice-rich crime novel, *Crooked Little Vein*, by Warren Ellis.

> I rifled the jacket for cigarettes, harvested one and went back to my chair. I swabbed some of the nicotine scum off the window behind the chair with the edge of my hand and peered down at my little piece of Manhattan.

The verbs leap out for me: *rifled, harvested, swabbed* … If he had replaced them with more serviceable verbs like "searched, grabbed, and wiped", they wouldn't have the same voice.

Here's another gorgeous sentence from Strand's memoir *The Body Is a Doorway*: "There's a memory I have that feels so spiderwebbed with sorrow and physical pain it's almost a dream."

"Spiderwebbed" is a brilliant adjective and, since the book often also references the natural world, a perfect one.

Passive Voice

If you've ever been told that conjugations of the verb "to be"—such as *am*, *was*, or *are*—read as "weak," that's somebody's way of suggesting you're writing in the passive voice, as opposed to the active voice. Constance Hale breaks verbs into "static" and "dynamic"—and the verb "to be" is notoriously static, she argues, lacking energy and stealing agency from your subjects.

In active voice, the subject *is* something or performs the action of the verb in the sentence.

The simplified active-voice formula is: [subject] + [verb (performed by the subject)] + [noun] = *Anita threw the softball.*

In a passive-voice construction, the subject of the clause *receives* the action of the verb. So the softball from the above sentence, which is receiving the action, becomes the subject.

The passive-voice formula: [subject] + [some form of the verb *to be*] + [past participle of a transitive verb] + [optional prepositional phrase]: *The softball was thrown by Anita.*

One of my favorite ways to "diagnose" if you're in the passive voice, according to Hamilton Education[1] is if you can add the phrase "by zombies" at the end of the phrase, it's probably passive voice. *The softball was thrown by zombies.*

Why is passive voice frowned upon? In nonfiction, journalism, or other writing in which it's important for the reader to know who is responsible, or the active agent of the action being described, passive voice makes that murky. It can make writing feel full of jargon, lacking concision, or removed. Politicians are notorious for passing the buck of responsibility through passive voice: "Tough decisions were made" (but not by me!). With the active voice, you don't let anyone off the hook.

On the other hand, sometimes passive voice may be authentic to your character's voice—just the way they talk, think, or write. In that case, go for it. As with all the suggestions in this book, and my passionate belief in, and love of, the fluidity of language—when you wield a technique intentionally, it can resonate with power or meaning.

AAVE and Intentional Variations Around the Verb "To Be"

There's one exception around the verb "to be" that's important to discuss here. Referring to earlier points about racism and classicism that are often embedded in language discussions, it's important to note (to non-Black writers, it probably goes without saying) that African American Vernacular English (AAVE) uses grammar patterns that have been stigmatized as incorrect but are not. In fact, AAVE's grammar rules are just a variation on structure from the anglophone grammar taught in most schools.

For example, "Standard English uses a conjugated be verb (called a copula) in a number of different sentences. (This may occur as is, 's, are, 're, etc.) In AAVE this verb is often not included," according to Jack Snidell, in a paper for the University of Hawaii[2].

For example, the anglophone sentence might read like this: *Some of them are big and some of them are small.*

While the AAVE version, with a null copula[3]—the verb removed—might read like this: *Some of them big and some of them small.*

Another example:

Anglophone: He is an expert.

AAVE: He an expert.

On this note, editor and sensitivity reviewer Stacey Parshall Jensen confirmed that non-Black writers should hesitate to use AAVE without a sensitivity or cultural review, too; it is all too easy to perpetuate a stereotype of Black people being ignorant. She wrote to me by email, "This usually appears when there is only one Black character among the white characters in a scene. The non-Black characters speak with proper grammar or with a relaxed, slightly slang vocabulary. But the Black character's dialogue overuses AAVE, and the impression left is the stereotype. This reveals a hidden or unconscious bias. A seasoned writer who has been immersed in the Black culture may not make this mistake, but these writers know how to create deeper, more authentic characters. Context, setting, and other characters should be considered when creating how a Black character sounds and moves through the world."

That may be more grammar than you wanted to explore, but the most important point of this section is to get you to look at your verbs and make them feel authentic to your characters.

Now, think about who your character / narrator is and what sides of them you want to show. Does your character walk or strut? Does your character throw or fling? Does your character get up or launch? Try to pick verbs that are true to their character.

Nouns

Perhaps the mere word "noun" conjures the phrase "a person, place, or thing," that little mnemonic you learned in an English class. Nouns aren't just structural pieces of your sentences, but key in shaping a writer's voice and tone. As we talk about specificity in nouns, you might have a faint memory of the terms "connotative" and "denotative" from ye olde English classes. A denotation is simply the concrete, dictionary definition of a word. For example, "dog" generically can be defined as a four-legged animal with a snout and a tail.

The connotative definition, however, refers to the more subjective and emotional associations that come with a word. For someone once bitten by a Doberman, "dog" might conjure terror. For another, it may conjure the joy of your French bulldog leaping for you with slobbering kisses when you come home at night. For yet someone else, it might suggest a man who is unfaithful to his partner.

So, when thinking of specificity and voice (moreover, tone), consider that nouns can change based on your character's or narrator's connotative associations of these words.

In another example, the denotation of "baby" might be an infant, a child. Yet "baby" can also be a term of endearment between two adults and even used as a form of harassment to diminish or assert power over a woman at a bar. "Hey, baby, I *said* you're beautiful."

The goal, then, is to think about the associations, values, and tone you're hoping to convey when you choose your words.

Specificity in Nouns

Vivid, concrete nouns can also help shape a distinctive voice. Bringing the lesson of specificity back to our example above, instead of a generic noun like *dog*, a more specific noun—labradoodle, mutt, or shaggy terrier—tells the reader more and subtly conveys tone and attitude.
For example:

- *The alley was full of dogs.* This is generic, somewhat neutral.
- *The alley was full of snarling Dobermans.* Now we have a sense of danger and tension.
- *The alley was full of yipping Chihuahuas.* This might evoke humor, a lighter tone.

Additionally, not all nouns are tangible objects; abstract nouns like *freedom*, *despair*, *love*, *regret*, and *ambition* are also nouns, though they speak less to concrete things a person can touch with their hands.

- A memoirist might use grief, nostalgia, loss to evoke an emotional tone.
- A journalist might rely on justice, corruption, accountability to convey authority and urgency.

Proper Nouns

Proper nouns can carry cultural or social weight and change, create, or reveal voice. For example:

- A big city versus Paris.
- A nun versus the Mother Superior
- The desert versus the Sahara

Compound Nouns and Voice

Compound nouns are those you bring together to create a deeper or more complex meaning. They're not better or worse than individual nouns; they can sometimes add layers of meaning and enhance voice. Consider the difference in tone in these compound nouns that all relate to entertainment:

- Formal: Award winner, film star, silver screen
- Conversational: Box-office smash, indie darling, Hollywood royalty
- Marketing speak: Fame machine, tabloid magnet, career killer

Adjectives and Adverbs

In the realm of annoying writing advice, a lot of instructors will tell you to rarely use adjectives or adverbs. I don't know if I just chafe against being told what to do, or I've seen the manifold ways language can be used to mold an experience, but I personally love a good adjective or adverb when used to achieve an effect. What really matters is that whatever effect happens on the page, it's there intentionally (or such a fabulous accident, it's worth keeping). If you're just slopping words on the page and not paying attention to how they connect to character and story, then yeah, probably your adjectives and adverbs aren't working well. But if you're being intentional, then use them how you will. A good friend of mine, Tomi Wiley James, once let me read her manuscript and a character's action was described as "pinkly" and I have never forgotten how perfectly and uniquely that adverb stood out for me.

Adjective Specificity

Adjectives and adverbs can sometimes create a more vivid voice through specificity too. Instead of a "big house," say a "sprawling estate." Instead of "walked quickly," try "strode." Stronger choices eliminate vagueness and enhance voice.

SYNTAX AND LEXICON

Unexpected or Invented Modifiers

Like my friend Tomi's adverb, "pinkly," you can really drum up voice when you break conventional expectations. A few of my favorite examples of unconventional modifiers come from Arundhati Roy's literary novel *The God of Small Things*: "Dinner-plate-eyed" and "Orangedrink Lemondrink Man."

In Ocean Vuong's poem *Torso of Air*, we have "gingerly bruised light."

And though not a modifier, per se, in Toni Morrison's novel *Beloved*, we have the character of Beloved asking Sethe to "Tell me your diamonds," a metaphor for something precious and ineffable that has been lost as much as actual diamonds.

Rhythm and Cadence

Adjectives and adverbs can also affect sentence flow, adding music and rhythm to a sentence. By the same token, as we'll discuss in Chapter 11, "Cutting Clutter," too many adjectives or adverbs can encumber sentences and their flow.

Refine in Revision

If any of this feels frustrating or difficult to access, it might help to think of voice as something you're carving out of the larger rock of your story in revision. Consider doing "voice waves" of edits—in which you go back and *only* edit for things like syntax, lexicon, and sentence flow, until you feel you've accurately captured your character's or narrator's voice.

In Summary

- **Syntax is architecture:** Syntax refers to the structure and organization of sentences, influencing how characters and narrators express themselves. Syntax can change between generations and for a variety of reasons.

- **Your natural syntax:** Every writer has an inherent way of structuring sentences based on their upbringing, culture, and experiences. You may need to adjust it when crafting distinct character voices.

- **Choose your verbs, adjectives, and nouns consciously:** Word choices shape voice, with verbs providing energy, adjectives adding specificity, and nouns grounding descriptions in vivid detail. The more concrete these are, the stronger your character's or narrator's voice may be.

- **Keep language fluid and inclusive:** Grammar rules should be viewed with an understanding of linguistic diversity, avoiding rigid enforcement that might suppress natural expression.

VOICE LESSONS

Writing Exercises

Now, you give it a try!

Syntax Remix

Take a paragraph from your current work in progress (or write a fresh one) and rewrite it in three different syntactical styles:

- Long, winding sentences (like John Green's *The Fault in Our Stars*)
- Short, clipped sentences (like Myriam Gurba's *English and Spanish*)
- Poetic or lyrical prose (like Tess Gunty's *The Rabbit Hutch*)

Compare the different versions and see what differences you find in the tone, rhythm, and voice of the piece.

Character Lexicon and Syntax Exploration

Write a short dialogue exchange between two characters who have very different backgrounds. Pay close attention to their syntax, vocabulary, and rhythm. Consider the following two options, or choose any of your own:

- One character with a formal, academic way of speaking.
- Another who uses slang, sentence fragments, or nonstandard grammar.

Then, rewrite the exchange from the perspective of a narrator who is eavesdropping on the conversation and has a totally different voice.

Power Verbs and Invented Modifiers

- Write a short scene using only strong, vivid verbs. Avoid generic verbs like "was," "walked," or "looked." Instead, choose words that evoke energy and character.
- Next, add unexpected adjectives or adverbs in a way that enhances the mood. Try inventing a modifier, like "pinkly" or "gingerly bruised light."
- Afterward, read your scene aloud. Does the language create a more distinctive and immersive voice?

> "We cannot direct the wind, but we can adjust the sails."
>
> —Dolly Parton

CHAPTER 8

Jargon, Slang, and Code-Switching

Voice and Context

Building characters from the ground up may feel like an impossible task if they're not based on someone you know, your own narrator, or otherwise drawn from a real person. Even considering all the elements we've looked at so far that comprise voice, it can sometimes be challenging to dial into a unique character voice.

In that regard, it can be useful to draw upon different contexts that may shape your character's voice, or places or conditions in which they spend a lot of time, such as a profession or job, a hobby, or a group of some kind. Say your character works in a hospital, is in the military, or is a diehard sports fan. These contexts may bleed over into their voice.

Additionally, in striving for realism in character voice, consider that characters may present one way in one context and an entirely different way in another, a phenomenon known as "code-switching" that everyone does to some extent, but some people may be forced to or feel pressure to do in greater amounts.

In this chapter, we'll look at how these things can add to shaping your character's voice.

Jargon

Jobs, hobbies, and clubs often have their own vernacular and jargon—words that you may only understand if you're "inside" that context or experience, they are part of the shorthand of that world, or they are technical terms required to understand a specific context. Additionally, these contexts can bleed over into regular life, so that a person at home may speak in the vernacular of work, only to find their family members looking quizzically at them. I'm going to put the examples first and see if you can pick up the context by the vernacular itself.

> The body. The-body-the-body-the-body, she thinks. Words lose their meaning when you repeat them. So do bodies, even in all their variations. Dead is dead. It's only the hows and whys that vary. Tick them off: Exposure. Gunshot. Stabbing. Bludgeoning with a blunt instrument, sharp instrument, no instrument at all when bare knuckles will do. Wham, bam, thank you,

ma'am. It's Murder Bingo! But even violence has its creative limits.

That excerpt comes from Lauren Beukes's supernatural crime novel *Broken Monsters*. The POV character is Gabriella, a police detective. Her thinking and word choice convey the jargon of her job. Even the cadence of her sentences is short, punchy, as though shaped by the often soul-killing work of her job. And because she spends so much of her life in her job, it becomes a part of her persona and voice.

Now let's look at another example, this one from Rachel Kushner's literary novel *Creation Lake*:

> I hear people, he said, whose voices are eternal in this underground world, which is all planes of time on a single plane.
>
> Here on earth is another earth, he said. A different reality, no less real. It has different rules.
>
> You won't understand any of this from me telling you about it, Bruno said. You might even dismiss what I say. The little I myself understand has taken patience, he said, and rigorous deprogramming.

In this passage, Sadie Smith (not her real name), an ousted FBI agent turned spy-for-hire, has received another email from a French philosopher named Bruno Lacombe, who has inspired a group of environmental "subversives" that she is tasked with infiltrating.

While not jargon, per se, Bruno's voice is forged in the language of his philosophical interests, always meandering and poetic, often seeming to be laced with deeper meaning. If anyone were to talk like this in a casual setting, say, over tea, you might think they were a little unique—or a professor.

One of the most jargon-filled spaces around is corporate culture, which creates a "language" that often stifles authenticity and feels sterile. I once asked people on my social media channels to tell me their least favorite jargon, and I wound up with several hundred, many of them "corporate-ese." Some least favorites of mine are:

- Circle back (to return to a topic)

- Move the needle (create measurable change)

- Out of pocket (away from my desk)

- Get granular (drill down to more nuanced discussion)

- Best practices (the most effective protocols to achieve a goal)

Why does this kind of jargon rub some of us the wrong way? I think it's because it squelches uniqueness and creative expression. If I have to say, "best practices" instead of "I've got some new ideas to improve things," I might also feel stifled in my suggestions. It also feels like it's derived from a capitalist ethos of "efficiency." *Say the most in the fewest words! Don't waste time expressing yourself! Get back to work!*

Slang

If the word slang makes you wrinkle your nose, you've probably been on the receiving end of someone's judgment about your phrasing, possibly someone who thinks they know the "proper" way of speaking or writing and is critical of your somehow informal, offhand, or otherwise "improper" usage.

But slang does not mean "improper"—rather, it refers to a manner of speaking or writing that allows for a commonality or shorthand among its users, one that is infused with subtext that members of a particular group would understand from a shared context. Most people use some kind of slang, be that each generation, people from different cultures, historical time periods, ethnic groups, and more. You can even think of slang as a subset of jargon.

There are also very classist and racist underpinnings to the judgment of slang. As Marquis Bey writes for the African American Intellectual History Society's website[4], *Black Perspectives*, "I am of the understanding that disdain for jargon or big words, or a demand for more accessible language, is at base a struggle over language and its effects. Who can use language, who is permitted to see themselves in language, who cannot, and what is language doing?"

Slang, then, is often seen as falling outside of accepted norms or traditions, when, in fact, a world without slang is a boring one, indeed. Bey adds, "What I'm suggesting is that the ideal of transparent, jargon-free, marvelously clear language disallows new, different things to be known and thought."

Slang can be thought of as an evolution of standards and norms that allows for creativity and individuality (hence, voice). Thus, getting in touch with your characters' slang can be freeing and allow you to enter a more authentic voice for your characters.

The simplest way to identify slang is to think of words or phrases that your character may say in a way that is offbeat, outside of dominant norms or culture, or specifically steeped within a specific culture or context (much like jargon).

In the book I've mentioned here a number of times because I love it so, *We Are All the Same in the Dark*, we're introduced to the character of Wyatt, whose slang and voice charms the heck out of me:

> She has a bad, bad mystery to her. I can feel it deep in the hollow of my spook bone, the one my dad broke when I was a kid. My arm is never wrong.

Slang often occurs when a character expresses themselves in a way that is less than, or more than, straightforward. It might be full of metaphor and simile, as it is above, or it might use phrases that are not directly explained or are not even literal, but which convey a better meaning, such as "spook bone" does here—you can take it to mean a kind of inner knowing, or to mean a specific part of his body, or both. For example, the non-slang way of saying this could have sounded like: "There's something mysterious about the girl. I have a strong intuition that is never wrong." There'd be nothing wrong with language like that, but it lacks the fullness of his unique voice.

Another example of slang comes from Leni Zumas's novel *Red Clocks*, about a time in the not-so-distant future (the book was published in 2018, it's worth noting), when abortion has become illegal and single mothers are about to lose their right to adopt and get in vitro fertilization (IVF). The character known as the biographer is at the gynecologist, hoping to start a round of IVF before the window closes. The nurse, whom she refers to here as Nurse Crabby and then just Crabby uses some fun slang as she prepares to draw the biographer's blood.

> "Let's go suck out some lineage."
>
> "Pardon?"
>
> "Anagram for blood."

Even though "anagram for blood" is incorrect (it's not an anagram), I like the way it gives unique voice to the character. The phrase "suck out some lineage" instead of draw blood is voicey and fun. Slang speaks to inherent creativity in people when they get bored or tired of the sameness of routine or want to freshen up the jargon they are forced to use.

Slang can also be exclusive, a way to gather people into an exclusive "club" or "group" like a sorority or academic group. You might have to know how to talk "like them" in order to be part of it.

As discussed in Chapter 7 on syntax and lexicon, the slang of each generation tends to change, too. My son, on the younger end of Gen Z at age seventeen, might say that something bad is "trash" and something awesome "slaps," that low enthusiasm or effort is "low-key" and that one thing being better than another or in a different context "hits different." I'm sure my son would roll his eyes if I whipped out the "rad," "bodacious," "gnarly," and "bitchin'" of my teen years in the 1980s. But it's worth noting that even *he* finds the slang of the kids younger than him, dubbed "Gen Alpha", to be cringe. Skibidi rizz in Ohio, anyone?

Code-Switching

Just as slang can reflect identity or belonging within a group, the way people adapt their language in different settings can also reveal a lot about character and influence voice. While slang is often used playfully or to reveal camaraderie or other connections, some people feel the need to actively alter their own authentic selves for the comfort of others.

This brings us to code-switching, a form of social navigation. Unlike slang, which is more of a tool of self-expression, code-switching can be a matter of survival, acceptance, or professional advancement. Code-switching is the act of adjusting one's speech, behavior, or even demeanor to conform with the "standards" of specific social situations. This is often done in ways that are designed to cater to the comfort or expectations of others, often in exchange for if not quite fair treatment, then at least *better* treatment, service, or employment opportunities.

Code-switching will be highly familiar to any minority group. As Marquis Bey pointed out, it is common "in spaces where negative stereotypes of Black people run counter to what are considered 'appropriate' behaviors and norms for a specific environment," such as Black students switching between standard English in the classroom or at work and African American Vernacular English (AAVE) with their peers and at home.

However, anyone can engage in code-switching. Women may try to toughen up and appear unemotional in a male-dominated work environment. Queer people may try to "pass" as straight in environments where their safety or identity feels threatened. People may even shift their behavior from context to context, such as behaving specific ways at work, with friends, with colleagues, even with family. Knowing when and how your character code-switches can also help a reader understand when they are being their authentic selves, and when they are "putting on" a manner of speech or behavior.

A classic example comes from the National Book Award-winning novel *James* by Percival Everett, a retelling of Mark Twain's novel *The Adventures of Huckleberry Finn* through the eyes of the enslaved character, Jim. Here, he's even given a code-switched name—he's James to his family and friends, but Jim to the white enslavers.

You'll notice quickly in the passage when and where James code-switches.

> I walked outside and over to the big fire, where the men were sitting. I was greeted and then I sat. We talked some about what happened to a runaway over at another farm.
>
> "Yeah, they beat him real good," Doris said.
>
> Doris was a man, but that didn't seem to matter to the slavers when they named him.

"All of them are going to hell," Old Luke said.

"What happened to you today?" Doris asked me.

"Nothing."

"Something must have happened," Albert said.

They were waiting for me to tell them a story. I was apparently good at that, telling stories. "Nothing, except I got carried off to New Orleans today. Aside from that, nothing happened."

"You what?" Albert said.

"Yes. You see, I thought I was drifting off into a nice nap about noon and the next thing I knew I was standing on a bustling street with mule-drawn carriages and whatnot all around me."

"You're crazy," someone said. I caught sight of Albert giving me the warning sign that white folks were close. Then I heard the clumsy action in the bushes and I knew it was those boys.

"Lak I say, I furst found my hat up on a nail. 'I ain't put dat dere,' I say to mysef. 'How dat hat git dere?' And I knew 'twas witches what done it. I ain't seen 'em, but it was dem. And one dem witches, the one what took my hat, she sent me all da way down to N'Orlins. Can you believe dat?" My change in diction alerted the rest to the white boys' presence. So, my performance for the boys became a frame for my story. My story became less of a tale as the real game became the display for the boys.

"You don't says," Doris said. "Dem witches ain't to be messed wif."

"You got dat right," another man said.

Let me be clear that there's nothing wrong with the way James and his Black friends speak in front of white people. They are leaning into a casual vernacular that the white people *judge* as "less than" and making themselves sound gullible to superstitions such as witches. However, it's the fact that it is unsafe for them to speak as they please *without repercussion* that forces them to subsume their intelligence, acumen, autonomy, and more. For enslaved Black people to demonstrate their intelligence during American chattel slavery was to risk their own lives. At the same time, the code-switching in the story reveals their superior survivor skills, which were necessary to survive the horrors and indignities of enslavement (and frankly, this necessity still persists today for many dealing with racism).

Another example comes from the Kushner novel above, in which our spy, Sadie Smith, presents herself as an American woman who has just come to France to get away. In this scene she meets her mark, Lucien Dubois, a man who can give her access to the group of "subversives" she's after. She will ultimately marry and betray him, all for her cause. He has no idea that she is not what she presents, a woman of average intelligence with no real goals or purpose. (The ellipses are mine to speed the passage along.)

> My initial contact with Lucien Dubois had been a cold bump. I had approached him in public, stranger to stranger ...
>
> I knew plenty about him, and that he had a kind of mannered affectation for old Paris, that he conceived of reality as stage-directed in black and white ...
>
> I sipped my drink. Lucien got an extra game. I sensed it was for me that he was playing so well ... Watching Lucien work the flippers, hold this machine on either side of its narrow end in order to guide the ball and control the game, it seemed to me that this posture, of man and machine, recalled some ancient form: a man behind the box that he steers–a plow, perhaps, or cart. Boys playing pinball in pantomime of an old world where men drove plows over fields, steered carts that were filled with hay or manure ...
>
> I don't waste my time on games. I don't know if this is because I'm not a man or because I'm not into games.

I love how her sharp intelligence comes through—you can even sense a hard-edged, predatory streak in her, a thrill at putting one over on him—her internal monologue revealing that she is not the affably benign woman she presents herself as.

While I don't encourage anyone to add jargon or slang to "voice up" a character if it isn't a natural fit, hopefully this chapter reinforces much of what we discussed in Chapter 1, that voice is shaped by so much of a character's identity and experiences. Language reflects the ways characters navigate with and within their community and their worlds. By paying close attention to techniques like jargon, slang, and code-switching, writers can hone voices that are as rich, nuanced, and complex as your characters.

In Summary

- **Character voice changes with context:** You can mine a character's profession, hobbies, and social circles for voice, as these influence the words they use and how they express themselves.

- **Jargon in language:** Professions, hobbies, and organizations often have their own specialized jargon that can seep into everyday speech, distinguishing outsiders from those "in the know."

- **Slang as expression and identity:** Slang, a shorthand and form of camaraderie, varies by generation, subculture, and social group, offering characters a unique way of expressing themselves and signaling belonging.

- **Code-switching for adaptation:** Code-switching is a way of intentionally speaking or behaving to navigate safely within traditional social spaces safely, and can affect voice.

- **Authenticity through speech patterns:** Through jargon, slang, or code-switching, a character can reveal their true self, their hidden fears, or the persona they project to the world.

VOICE LESSONS

Writing Exercises

Now, you give it a try!

Exploring Jargon

Create a character who works in a specific profession, hobby, or group (a doctor, athlete, artist, or tech expert). Write a scene in which they use the jargon of their field in conversation with a non-expert (such as a family member or friend) who is baffled, amused, or challenged by it. Focus on how the jargon shapes the character's voice and how the non-expert reacts to it.

Code-Switching Scene

Write a scene where your character code-switches between two distinct environments (at work and at home, with friends and with authority figures, or the like). Show the change in their language, tone, and behavior. Pay attention to why they switch and how the switch reveals something about their identity or social pressures.

Slang and Voice

Choose a specific group or subculture (teenagers, musicians, a certain regional group) and create a character who speaks in their slang. Write a dialogue-heavy scene in which this character interacts with someone who doesn't understand their slang. Focus on how slang conveys the character's identity, and how the confusion or connection between characters can highlight their differences or similarities.

> "Voice is always pushing at the edges of genre, swinging from the boundaries like a jungle gym. The limitation of genre can give voices a place to play."
>
> —Sonya Huber, *Voice First: A Writer's Manifesto*

CHAPTER 9

How Genre Shapes Voice

What Is Genre?

As much as publishers would like us to believe that genre is a hallowed and natural way of categorizing books, as though books organically collect on shelves together like flocks of birds, genre is at root a marketing strategy, a way of categorizing stories to direct reader expectations and dollars. However, publishing has been successful at conditioning readers to expect books to fall into these neat little categories, so when you hit the bookstore, you will likely travel to one of the sections that houses your favorites.

Moreover, many of these genres do have expectations of voice and tone associated with them, so that when you crack the cover or download the e-book of a cozy mystery, you don't get a noir thriller or madcap rom-com instead.

While a wide variety of subgenres has emerged, which I'll talk about a bit further down, some of the most common / popular genres you'll find include:

- Mystery or Thriller
- Romance
- Science Fiction
- Fantasy
- Historical
- Horror
- Literary
- Young Adult / Middle Grade variations on these themes

Voice Before Genre

Many writers don't think about genre—they just write, and personally, I'm a fan of discovery over dictation, of launching into a story first and then finding out what genre it might fit if you're not already genre-focused. You might have chosen your genre more specifically than that too, as a fan of, say, romantasy (subgenre alert!) or psychological suspense. My only caveat is that if your deep and abiding desire is to publish within a strict genre, such as sweet Westerns, you will absolutely have to hew to the expectations of that genre's voice and tone if you hope to

HOW GENRE SHAPES VOICE

be traditionally published within it. Even if you take an alternate publishing path, readers of that genre will come looking for the voice they already expect.

Guess the Genre

Now, let's look at several examples drawn from some of the more traditional genres here and try to guess what genre they're from, then look at what the tells are. I'm going to put the book title and author name at the bottom of each passage too, so it doesn't lead you on.

> What is it that tugs at her mind? The feel of it is irritating, gummy, as if something is caught in her hair and needs to be yanked free. The sensation is centered in her sessapinae—no. Deeper. This tugs at the light of her spine, the silver between her cells, the threads that bind her to the ground and to Found Moon and to Schaffa and to the sapphire that hovers just above the clouds of Jekity, visible now and again when the clouds break a little. The irritation…is…it is … north.
>
> Something is happening up north.

What genre do you think this is? Why?

My students often think this is either science fiction or fantasy, and they're sort of both right. It's billed as fantasy, and it is truly an astonishment of world building and imagined possibilities, yet author N.K. Jemisin's work—in this case, the first in her Broken Earth trilogy, *The Fifth*

Season, is so detailed and nuanced, you can almost imagine that her creations are possible in a distant future.

The clues that at first give away the genre to my students are words like "sessapinae," "Found Moon," and "Jekity"—which sound not quite of this world. The way the character seems to be able to sense things that are happening is also a clue.

Now let's look at another example and try to identify its genre:

> The case comes in, or anyway it comes in to us, on a frozen dawn in the kind of closed-down January that makes you think the sun's never going to drag itself back above the horizon. Me and my partner are finishing up another night shift, the kind I used to think wouldn't exist on the Murder Squad: a massive scoop of boring and bigger one of stupid, topped off with an avalanche of paperwork. Two scumbags decided to round off their Saturday night out by using another scumbag's head for a dance mat, for reasons that are clear to no one including them; we turned up six witnesses, every one of whom was banjoed drunk, every one of whom told a different story from the other five and every one of whom wanted us to forget the murder case and investigate why he had been thrown out of the pub / sold bad skunk / ditched by his girlfriend.

I'm going to bet that even without the hint of "Murder Squad" you'd already know this was crime fiction of some kind. Could be mystery, could be thriller, but while that's not yet clear, what do we already notice about the voice?

One thing that shows up time and time again in crime fiction is that detectives, cops, first responders, and those who encounter the spoils of crime over and over tend to develop a somewhat jaded-sounding voice—unless they're a newbie, of course. And detective Stephen Moran in Tana French's mystery novel *The Trespasser* is no exception. However, his voice is not *just* jaded; it's also slightly amused. He's fond of a good simile—anthropomorphizing the cold January and the sun as though they're another couple of drunks he's dragged in off the street. He even gives the dull slog of paperwork a lively little description as "a massive scoop of boring and a bigger one of stupid."

Where his cynicism starts to show through the cracks is when he describes the night's events and the people in it in a way that suggests he's lost his compassion for the people involved. The people are all "scumbags" and not too bright by the way he describes them. This kind of weary-on-the-job voice and tone is not uncommon in crime fiction.

For our last example here, the only context I'll give you is this: a Blackfoot Indian man has a guilty conscience about once shooting a pregnant elk on a hunting trip. After stumbling across a part of its hide he'd forgotten he had, he begins to have visions of it:

> While she's gone Lewis looks over the top of the fan, at the gouge the ladder left in the wall of the living room. The new wound in the house. Moving there like an afterimage, like it was left behind, is just trying to

creep past without being seen, he's ninety percent sure there's the shadow of a person up against that wall. A thin shadow, just for a flicker of a moment. A woman with a head that's not human. It's too heavy, too long. When it turns as if to fix him in its wide-set eyes, he raises his hand to block her vision, to hide, but it's too late. It's been too late for ten years already. Ever since he pulled that trigger.

A few words instantly strike me in this passage: "gouge," "wound," "creep." These feel like foreshadowing and they're tonally in line with the genre. In addition, we have some freaky imagery of a woman "with a head that's not human" and when she turns to look at him, "it's too late."

It's possible to think of this as a thriller or even something just vaguely paranormal, but I think most people will sense that this novel, *The Only Good Indians*, by Stephen Graham Jones, is horror.

Of course, most of the time you pick up a book, you already know what genre it is—so while the genre may not be a surprise, it's helpful to be intentional with voice choices that match the genre you're writing in.

Reader Expectations vs. Authorial Freedom

Voice is a powerful tool in establishing genre expectations, but you can absolutely and deliberately subvert those expectations if you do so with intention and care.

To subvert genre expectations, you first need to know what the genre expectations are, which means reading widely in that genre or studying it. And of course, there's the question of why you are subverting it. A thriller steeped in humor might allow a reader to handle a scary or difficult subject, perhaps.

An example of this is a book by Brittany Newall, called *Soft Core,* which you might expect to be erotica (by the title alone) and with its frank descriptions of sex, yet it is more of a literary character study of longing and loss, of how we fulfill human desires in manifold ways. It's full of lyrical writing and deeply personal character dives.

> Now, in the diner, as the fluorescent lights played up her scars and the odor of cooking oil cut through her perfume, I studied the girl to whom all these things had first belonged. The lilac bed, the lying man. She had no idea that I'd sullied them both, my longing like an automated sprinkler wetting everything in its path. She thought of me, preposterously, as a friend. She was chatty and relaxed as she dug into her cheesecake.

While genre-as-marketing-tool may make genres seem definitive, the truth is that many genre rules aren't as rigid as they seem. If you're going to straddle genres, be sure that you're truly inhabiting both genres in your language and voice so it doesn't come across as a series of jarring tone shifts.

Straddling Genre and Subgenre

While it may be true that some genres have stricter expectations of voice than others, the truth is there are probably more subgenres than standard ones, as well as lots of genre crossovers that allow for fun and play with voice and tone shifts. Some examples:

- Tana French writes literary mysteries. They're equally as character driven as plot driven, with an emphasis on language, too.

- Victor LaValle writes supernatural stories such as *The Changeling* and *Lone Women* that masquerade as genre like horror or fantasy while exploring larger social issues.

- Diana Gabaldon, author of the *Outlander* series, among others, writes romance novels that do double time as historical and even literary fiction.

- Carl Hiaasen, author of books like *Bad Monkey* and *Skinny Dip*, writes comedic mysteries.

Where the voice / genre match-up really matters is when you're pitching to agents or editors who have specific requests and guidelines.

There are other categories that can help you fall outside of genre, such as "upmarket," "high concept," or "contemporary" fiction.

Genre Straddlers

If you are a writer whose work doesn't fit neatly into a genre box or straddles genres, that is perfectly okay. It could make your work more appealing to readers who are looking for something new or different. Moreover, sometimes finding your voice means finding yourself between genres. If you *must* choose one, for marketing purposes, choose the genre that speaks to the largest theme / most content in your work. Or you might find a subgenre that speaks to you: paranormal romance, urban fantasy, cozy mystery.

Breaking Genre

I have a personal soft spot for books that do more than just straddle genre but break it altogether; they are hard to define or quantify, and I'm a fan of anything that can't be easily pinned down. While publishing often lobs these all into the bin marked "literary," there are books in which I'd say *voice* is itself the genre. These stories may be driven more by the character or narrator voice than any structural elements that prop up other genres. There may be a Greek chorus of voices, voices of the dead or ghosts, unreliable narrators, snippets or vignettes of memory, and so on.

Here are a few examples from books I loved, whose voices almost immediately sank their literary teeth into me and dragged me through the thicket of their sentences, their rich character experiences, and more. These books might have a genre stamped on their sides, but that category is but a mere suggestion in most cases.

From Rene Denfeld's novel, *The Enchanted*:

> This is an enchanted place. Others don't see it but I do.
>
> I see every cinder block, every hallway and doorway. I see the doorways that lead to the secret stairs and the stairs that take you into stone towers and the towers that take you to windows and the windows that open to wide clean air. I see the chamber where the cloudy medical vines snake across the floor, empty and waiting ...[*I've excised key details to let a question linger in your mind that we'll address in the Tone section*]. I see the soft-tufted night birds as they drop from the heavens. I see the golden horses as they run deep under the earth, heat flowing like molten metal from their backs.

The voice is insistent. It sweeps you along rivers of sentences that reach wavelike peaks. It's a voice that seems both childlike and insistent, as if it is begging you to see things from its perspective instead of your own, instead of the starker truths the novel will reveal.

Another favorite is from Steven Dunn's novel *Potted*

Meat, a novel told in a child-turned-teen's vignettes in his West Virginia town "as he struggles with abusive parents, poverty, alcohol addiction, and racial tensions," as the back cover suggests. Dunn said he strove to write as close to a child's voice as he could, allowing the sentence structure and thought patterns to be true to that:

Happy Little Trees

> Bob Ross is on. He has paint. I don't. First I grind flowers with a rock but it don't work. I chew and chew dandelions. Spit mixes into yellow paste. I chew grass. I chew mulberries. I chew wild onions. They don't make color so I swallow. Tingles back of the neck and waters my eyes. Chew coal. Chew red clay. Chew what a grasshopper chews. I chew a grasshopper. Crunchy, then juice squirts to the back of throat. The paste is chunky brown green white. Lick off hand and chew until smooth. Open jar, chew lightning bugs. Wait till night when they light, then rip off the ass, smear it on my face.

I love the way the voice takes us through the act of discovery itself, the character making "paint" from the world around him, the combination of shorter and longer sentence fragments creating a rhythm that feels remarkably like the act of putting a paintbrush to a canvas.

Most importantly, trust your own instincts on voice first before you try to force yourself into a genre-based voice "box." Voice can be refined and revised more intimately as you get to know your characters and the story, so don't be afraid to play.

In Summary

- **Use voice to establish genre:** Pay attention to word choice, sentence rhythm, and point of view to align with the reader's expectations for your genre.

- **Voice before genre:** Write freely, then step back and analyze how your voice naturally aligns with genre conventions. Adjust as needed to fit (or break) expectations.

- **Subvert genre with intention:** If you're bending the rules of voice and tone, make sure you're doing it intentionally and with balance.

- **Anchor the reader:** Even if your story bends genre norms, give the reader a clear starting point so they know what kind of experience they're in for. A strong opening with a defined voice helps set the tone.

- **If your book resists a single genre, highlight its strongest theme:** When pitching agents or marketing your book, focus on the primary emotional or narrative drive—whether it's suspense, romance, or mystery—even if your voice pulls from multiple genres.

- **Compare your voice:** Read widely in your genre (and beyond) to analyze how authors shape voice to meet genre expectations.

- **If voice is your strongest asset, lean into it:** Some books, especially literary fiction, defy traditional genre categorization because the voice itself is the defining feature. If that's your strength, don't be afraid to let it lead the story.

VOICE LESSONS

Writing Exercises

Now, you give it a try!

Genre Identification and Voice Shift

Step 1: Take a scene from your story that is in its original genre (cozy mystery, romance, literary, or even "unsure").

Step 2: Write a paragraph that reflects the tone, voice, and style typical of that genre. For example, if it's a cozy mystery, the voice may be lighthearted and witty. If it's literary fiction, the tone might be more introspective and philosophical.

Step 3: Now, rewrite the scene in a completely different genre. Change the tone, voice, and pacing to match a new genre (make it darker and more suspenseful, or inject humor and light romance).

Genre Expectations vs. Personal Voice

Step 1: Write a scene in which your character or narrator is aware of or struggling with the genre they are in. For memoirists, try to play up possible "genre tropes" within your true story. For instance, in a romance genre (or a romantic theme in memoir), your character might be frustrated by how the tropes are playing out (or resisting them). If you're writing a thriller, they might comment on the clichéd nature of a dangerous chase scene.

Step 2: Have the character's personal voice—whether humorous, rebellious, or cynical—clash with or intentionally fit into the expectations of their genre. For example, in a romance, they might crack jokes about "falling for the brooding stranger" or in a horror novel, they might question why they're going into a dark basement despite all the warnings.

Genre Fusion and Subgenre

Step 1: Pick two genres or subgenres to combine. If you're a memoir writer, even better! How can you give your memoir a noir mystery feel, or turn it into a fantasy? For fiction writers, you could merge romantasy with a sweet Western, or sci-fi with mystery.

Step 2: Write a short scene where these genres overlap. This could be a character navigating a love triangle in a fantasy world set in the past, or a detective uncovering an alien conspiracy in a future dystopia.

Step 3: Focus on how the tropes and conventions of both genres can play off each other. For example, you could create a scene in which a romance subplot happens against the backdrop of a space-exploration mystery or a historical romance laced with magical realism.

"When I cannot see words curling like rings of smoke round me I am in darkness—I am nothing."

—Virginia Woolf, *The Waves*

CHAPTER 10

Making Sentences Sing: Rhythm and Musicality

The Music of Voice

I am a sucker for a voice so full of sounds and imagery that I can almost crunch it between my teeth or sweep its velvet against my skin. Others may prefer serviceable sentences that get the job done without any flourish. While voice runs the gamut from the perfunctory to the poetic, sound is a key piece of its creation. It may seem weird to talk about sound when talking about writing, given that it is a medium we often consume with our eyes. Yet, this is the magic of language—it is auditory, it is visual, it is as kinetic as American Sign Language, and as tactile as Braille. It's made to be read and heard and sung and spoken and rapped. Words and, in fact, the letters and letter combinations that make up words, have energies and frequencies that can make sentences into music.

In this chapter, we'll look at a few techniques of rhythm and musicality in language as ways to give texture to voice, or to stretch a little deeper into what makes your characters' or narrator's voices unique. The more intentional you are with sentences, the more directly you can shape voice to do your bidding.

Lyricism

I am a big fan of lyrical writing, but not everyone likes it. Sometimes people like the prose to step out of the way of the story; but me, I like writing that is a little rich with technique. As Emma Darwin writes in her blog "This Itch of Writing,"[5] "Lyrical writing wears its poetic techniques a little more on its sleeve than your prose does the rest of the time. That's not just rhythm / sound / repetition / rhyme / pattern / echo, but also figurative language: metaphor, simile and images."

It's important to discuss the uses of imagery in lyricism. We'll also look at how lyrical voices utilize many of the strategies we'll talk about in this chapter, from alliteration to metaphor and simile to other kinds of devices.

Imagery can sometimes detract from pain or horror in the content of a story, or take a philosophical tone, as Erika Krouse uses it in the reported memoir, *Tell Me Everything*, which details her helping a lawyer investigate a high-profile rape case involving a football team at a well-known university. Krouse relies upon metaphors and similes that are thematically linked to the subject of her story. The lines are also aesthetically lovely and pleasing to speak aloud:

> Power bounced off the eggshell-finish walls and throbbed from the light fixtures, and none of that power was for me.

And:

> Tree trunks splayed across the ground, piles of enormous pick-up sticks. Live soldiers held up the many dead.

There's a lot of extra space given to imagery in this book because it is such a rich way to deepen, enhance, and even create voice.

Dialect

Dialect, speech that's unique to a region or social group, can feel rhythmic and dynamic, especially when it is different from your own. I love to read dialect, though there are few that I would be able to authentically capture myself.

Here's another example from Steven Dunn's novel *Potted Meat*, where the characters are steeped in a West Virginian dialect that's rich and full of movement:

> Boy get that paper and read me all the dead folks, this

old woman's eyes getting bad and this ol' Arthur got my fingers all bent up. While you over here, help me get these neckbones to boiling ...

In another example, renowned writer Zora Neale Hurston had the rare opportunity to interview one of the last known survivors of a transatlantic slave ship. Cudjo Lewis was eighty-six at the time Huston visited him in 1927. She took down his story and transcribed it in his own words, which was only published as its own book in 2018, titled *Barracoon*. Lewis's voice is rich in Alabama dialect with the essence of his own childhood in Africa.

> My people in Afficky, you unnerstand me, dey not rich. Dass de truth, now. I not goin' tellee you my folks dey rich and come from high blood. Den when you go in de Afficky soil an' astee de people, dey say, 'Why Kossula over dere in Americky soil tellee de folks he rich? I tellee you lak it tis. Now, dass right, ain' it?

Dialect in memoir can be a beautiful thing, especially if it's familiar enough to you that you're capturing it accurately, much as Huston does in *Barracoon*. Dialect is a lot trickier to pull off in fiction if you aren't immersed in the dialect your characters are using. It's easy to miss the nuances that truly make dialect so rich and wonderful, and to create stereotypes, parody, or inaccuracies that can be interpreted as racism or bigotry.

What makes dialects so wonderful when they're done right, though, is that they are often steeped in very specific elements of our identity and being: a place, a cultural heritage, a time period, and more.

Alliteration

Alliteration is one of those devices that, when used sparingly or intentionally, can bring energy and musicality to a sentence, but when used too heavily can start to clutter a sentence or paragraph.

In a nutshell, alliteration is a form of consonance, or repeating consonant sounds in adjacent words, even if they have different vowel sounds or assonance, repeating vowel sounds.

My first alliterative awakening was to the poetry of Gerard Manley Hopkins in high school English class. Though I might not have connected to the content of his poetry, I liked the way it made reading tactile, even synesthetic, like I could feel the shapes of the letters in my mouth as much as read or hear them. Here's the beginning of his poem, "The Windhover":

> I caught this morning morning's minion, king-
>
> dom of daylight's dauphin, dapple-dawn-drawn Falcon, in his riding
>
> Of the rolling level underneath him steady air, and striding
>
> High there, how he rung upon the rein of a wimpling wing

> In his ecstacy! then off, off forth on swing,
>
> As a skate's heel sweeps smooth on a bow-bend: the hurl and gliding
>
> Rebuffed the big wind. My heart in hiding
>
> Stirred for a bird,—the achieve of, the mastery of the thing!

The alliteration here enables the reader to feel as though they *are* the bird catching wind, flying, experiencing the world through its wings. All I know is that my inner ear feels like it's tap dancing on cobblestones when I read alliteration. Maybe someone else's brain experiences it as jarring, but it's fun to play with when you can make it work in a way that doesn't pull the reader out of the experience.

Not only is alliteration pleasurable to the ears and brain, but studies have also shown it helps memory retention, a fun fact.[6]

Alliteration can also create a sense of movement, energy, and emotion, as in this example from the great Maya Angelou's novel, *I Know Why the Caged Bird Sings*:

> Up the aisle, the moans and screams merged with the sickening smell of woolen black clothes worn in summer weather and green leaves wilting over yellow flowers.

There's a crowded and oppressive energy to all the m's and s's in the first half of the sentence, then relieved a little in the l's and w's of the second half of the sentence.

Yet another version is among my favorites. This example is from the novel *Winter's Bone* by Daniel Woodrell:

> The world seemed huddled and hushed and her crunching steps cracked loud as ax whacks. As she crunched past houses built on yon slopes yard dogs barked faintly from under porches but none came into the cold to make a run at her and flash teeth.

Here, we interweave a bit of onomatopoeia, that long and complex description for when a word describes or sounds like the thing it seeks to describe, such as *buzz* or *sizzle*. Here, the consonant shushing of "*hu*ddled" coupled with the sibilance of "hu*sh*ed" mimic those softer actions and sounds, while the hard consonant sounds "*cr*unching," "*cr*a*ck*ed" and "*ax* wh*ack*s" offer the sounds of those harsh steps. These words beautifully create an auditory experience of hearing someone's steps interrupting the quiet with their intrusive presence.

One more example comes from Terese Marie Mailhot's memoir *Heart Berries*, about a Native American woman coming of age on the Seabird Island Indian Reservation. This example straddles the realms between alliteration and simply being rhythmic. As I read it with my eyes, I realized that in my head, I was hearing it as either slam poetry or rap because of its gorgeous rhythm:

> You had a hard-on for my oratory. Some of my stories were fabricated. I had authority—a thing that people like you haven't witnessed.

Oratory. Stories. Authority. The rhythm could be set to drums.

Consonance / Assonance

If alliteration is largely composed of consonance, then another feature of musicality is assonance, the repetition of vowel sounds, often found in rhyming but not exclusively. Here's an example from Shakespeare's Sonnet No. 1: "His tender heir might bear his memory."

The "eh" sound in "tender," "heir," "bear," and "memory" create a soft, breathy quality that matches the content of a "tender heir."

Here's another from *The God of Small Things* by Arundhati Roy: "Dead leaves flitted lightly over the ground, scattering their brittle, browned shadows."

Here, the short "i" sound matches the qualities of the leaves, with "flitting" and "brittle" rhyming in a way that mimics movement. Not to mention, small "i" sounds often connote "little" things, according to Constance Hale in *Sin and Syntax*.

Parallelism

Another fun literary device you can use when shaping voice is parallelism, where grammatical structures or patterns, similar in form or content, are juxtaposed or repeated within a sentence or passage to create rhythm, reinforce ideas, and build momentum.

You can use it to create rhythm and musicality, like Toni Morrison does in her novel *Beloved*: "In this place, we flesh; flesh that weeps, laughs; flesh that dances on bare feet in grass."

Morrison's parallel repetition of "flesh that weeps" and "flesh that dances" not only creates a kind of musicality and thematic resonance, but it also enhances the humanity of the people her narrator is describing.

You might also use parallelism to emphasize an idea or intensify a meaning, like this example from Barack Obama's memoir, *Dreams from My Father*:

> "I knew that there were good men and bad men, that there were fair laws and unfair ones, and that a president could do what he wanted if enough people didn't care."

These contrasts framed by clauses beginning with "that"—"that there were good men..." and "that there were fair laws..." create a rhythm driving us to a point with impact—that a president can get away with bad things if "enough people didn't care."

You might also use parallelism to demonstrate the similarities or contrasts between relationships, as Charles Dickens does in the classic opening to *A Tale of Two Cities*:

It was the best of times, it was the worst of times; it was the age of wisdom, it was the age of foolishness ...

Once again, the pairing of opposites creates an interesting rhythm, but it also highlights irony here, as he comments upon the contradictions of the era.

Repetition, Anaphora, and Epistrophe

While repetition can clutter a sentence on the one hand, and might need cutting (see Chapter 11), conscious word choice or phrase repetition can create a fabulous rhythm.

An elegant example comes from "The Dead," a short story by James Joyce: "His soul swooned slowly as he heard the snow falling faintly through the universe and faintly falling, like the descent of their last end, upon all the living and the dead."

The repetition, with a twist, of "falling faintly" and "faintly falling" mimics the pattern of snowfall, as does the consonance of all the s's and w's juxtaposed with the assonance of the "oos" and "ows" in "swooned slowly". It slows the reader down to zoom in on this potent emotional moment for the character and creates a focused hush.

Another beautiful example is how the poet Amanda Gorman, who performed her poem *The Hill We Climb* at Joe Biden's presidential inauguration, uses a form of repetition known as anaphora, a repetition of a word or phrase at the *beginning* of a sentence (ellipses are mine): "We will rise from the gold-limbed hills of the west...We will rise from the windswept northeast... We will rebuild, reconcile, and recover."

This is not to be confused with "epistrophe," in which a word or phrase is repeated at the *end* of a clause, something you might find frequently in song lyrics or poetry. One example comes from a powerful poem by Brian Bilston called "America Is a Gun." Each quatrain ends with the titular phrase, a poem excoriating gun violence in the U.S.

> England is a cup of tea.
>
> France, a wheel of ripened brie.
>
> Greece, a short, squat olive tree.
>
> America is a gun.
>
> Brazil is football on the sand.
>
> Argentina, Maradona's hand.
>
> Germany, an oompah band.
>
> America is a gun.

Repetition can enhance or clutter a sentence, depending on how you use it, but it can be delightfully rhythmic and creative when you use it intentionally in creating voice.

Word Sounds and Colors

As I said early on, I am not a linguist, but there's so much I love about linguistics when my brain manages to parse it out into digestible bites.

I've gained a lot from Reuven Tsur, a "literary theorist" in his book *What Makes Sound Patterns Expressive.* He offers up what he calls "cognitive poetics" about the sounds and even "colors" of words and their parts. He writes that his book, "[T]akes its departure from the 'mysterious' intuitions laymen, poets, and academic investigators have about the perceptual qualities and emotional symbolism of speech sounds."

It's a compelling idea, that *sounds themselves* evoke emotions, which anyone who has ever heard music knows to be true. Though, it's one you might not have thought about applying to the written word.

The next section attempts to distill down some of the essentials of his work from his heady academic tome that may be the most useful to you at the sentence-refining level. Here are a few thoughts:

Consonants Carry Emotional Potential

Stop thinking of your consonants as merely letters, Tsur encourages. Consonants exert significant influence on the feeling (tone) of a piece of writing, some producing what he terms "gentleness" and others "aggression" due to their acoustic qualities.

"Tender sounds," are typically smooth, continuous, and melodious—like vowels, liquids (l's) and nasals (m, n). These sounds, Tsur suggests, convey warmth, openness, and emotional softness.

"Aggressive" sounds, in contrast, can feel abrupt, noisy, and sharp, such as *t* and *k*. They can also convey strength, rigidity, or harshness. (Think about how many swear words have a hard consonant stop. Fuck. Shit. Crap.)

Double-Edged Sounds

While some sounds may be more obviously "tender" or "aggressive" (those descriptions charm me), some consonants, such as *d* and *g*, can play either role, depending on the context, Tsur says. Poets and writers may have an intuitive grasp of the emotional context of a sound, while others may need to work harder to construct them.

It presents you with a way to deliberately choose consonants that reflect the tone or emotional nuance you wish to create.

Vowel Sounds

If consonants are "streams of energy obstructed to some degree," Tsur writes, then vowels are "uninterrupted streams of energy." I love the idea of sounds as energy.

He also suggests that vowels can be "bright" or "dark,"

based on their acoustic resonance, created by distinct combinations of overtones. This "shading" is created by how you move your mouth to make the sounds. When vowels resonate closer to the front of your mouth, their overtones are different from vowels that resonate toward the back. Thus, front vowels produce a more "bright" or "open" auditory texture, while back vowels produce something "darker" or more muted.

He breaks it down like so:

- **Front vowels (/i/, /e/)**: often suggest brightness, sharpness, clarity, or lightness.

- **Back vowels (/u/, /o/)**: suggest darkness, depth, warmth, or mystery.

For example, a line containing mostly front vowels like "keen," "gleam," and "bright" will feel sharper, lighter, and more alert than one heavy in back vowels like "loom", "gloom," and "moon," which evoke a moodier, deeper, or darker emotional atmosphere.

Each vowel has a distinctive "formant," a unique concentration of acoustic energy at specific frequencies. Imagine these as different patches of light and shade—our ears pick up these subtle differences and translate them subconsciously into emotional textures:

- **Front vowels (/ee/, /ay/)**: These vowels resonate higher up in frequency, making them feel lighter, brighter, and more energized.

- **Back vowels (/oo/, /oh/):** These vowels resonate lower, creating a more muted, darker, calmer feeling.

Thus, if you agree with his characterization, you can deliberately choose vowel patterns to reinforce a mood, tone, or feeling.

Poetic Implications

Tsur's explanation of vowel color can provide you with an extra set of tools for shaping voice and tone. When you want a scene to feel intimate, tender, or lighthearted, lean toward front vowels. If your aim is mystery, gravity, melancholy, or seriousness, consider back vowels.

Mixing vowel sounds strategically within sentences or passages can add contrast and tension. And don't fret—it's not something that comes intuitively to most of us and is often a craft level best saved for revision.

Interesting Word Choices

As writers, you are tasked with dropping readers into your stories without them noticing the process, while at the same time, allowing them to admire the ingredients. Don't you love it when a word piques your interest or curiosity, glimmering within a passage? As discussed in the specificity chapter, the more deeply you think about your character, the more specific you can be with the words you use.

Interesting word choices wake readers up, intriguing them and keeping them riveted to the sentence. One of my favorite short-story writers, Lorrie Moore, does this often in the stories from her book *Self Help:* "At work you will be lachrymose and distracted. You will shamble through the hall like a legume with feet. People will notice."

While some of us may have to look up *lachrymose*, I like it for the way it sounds alone. And how great is *shamble* as a verb? Not walk, not shuffle, *shamble*. A *legume* with feet? This is full of voice, built with interesting words.

What makes for an interesting word will vary, of course, from writer to writer—and will depend upon such factors as your native language and country of origin. Words are imbued with the complexity of things, such as the effects of colonization or the pain of not having been allowed to speak your "true" language.

Vary Sentence Length and Cadence

Returning to author Jane Alison's description of reading as a "felt motionless movement," you may be familiar with the way that sentence length contributes to rhythm and cadence that you can hear in your inner ear when you read (or literally, if listening to an audiobook). When every sentence is the same length, for example, it can sound monotonous or academic. If you have too many short sentences in a row, it may feel choppy, like riding a horse and buggy over a broken road. Too many long or run-on sentences in a row might make the reader feel as though they need to take a breath. Attention to sentence length can help you keep your voice from feeling constricted or lax or, on the other hand, if that is the effect you're going for, it can help you intentionally create those effects.

It's very hard to prescribe sentence lengths and cadence, but a good variety can offer nice musicality. Here's an example that combines sentence lengths to mix up the rhythm:

"He careened down the face of the hill, his tires juddering madly over roots and rocks. Rocks. Like the one that had cracked his parents' windshield. Killed them in minutes. One damn rock had changed his whole life."

The first sentence is longer—it moves sort of like a person riding a bike down a hill might. Then a short, one-word sentence: "Rocks." It's like a pause, or a period at the end of the sentence. The next three sentences are longer than one word, but shorter than the beginning sentence. A nice variety that allows the paragraph to flow.

Paying attention to how your sentences flow and even "feel" in your mouth and inner ear helps to create the rhythm you're going for.

An Economy of Words

Though I clearly have a bias for imagery and more complicated sentence texture, plenty of writers deliver a powerful voice or tone punch through much sparer language or syntax. One of my favorite "spare" writers is novelist R.O. Kwon, who writes with such economy, you get the feeling that not a single word is wasted or out of place.

Notice how she also utilizes a variety of sentence lengths, some as short as a few words, in her novel *The Incendiaries*, in which a bright young college student named Phoebe is drawn into a religious sect with a violent ideology by a charismatic leader while her well-meaning boyfriend, Will, tries to keep from losing her.

> The Phipps building fell. Smoke plumed, the breath of God. Silence followed, then the group's shouts of triumph. Wine glasses clashed together, flashing martial light. He sang the first bars of a Jejah psalm. Others soon joined in. Carillon bells chimed, distant birds blowing white, strewn, like dandelion tufts, an outsize wish.

Not only does every word feel intentional, but the energy of the paragraph is also hurried and urgent, matching the action of an orchestrated explosion, until we get to that final sentence. Then that comma-separated list slows us down, as though our parachute has opened after a terrifyingly swift descent out of the sky.

Intentional Sentence Fragments

When used intentionally, sentence fragments can be a stylistic way to create a particular effect. On one hand, they can create a sharp, shotgun-like energy to the sentence, and on the other hand, they can create a dreamy or surreal experience.

Similarly, intentional sentence fragments and short, clipped sentences can bring drama, immediacy, or even shock to a moment. Like staccato music notes, they can have a physiological impact on the reader—speeding your heart rate or breathing, creating tension, or building intensity.

Here's an example from Chuck Wendig's supernatural novel *Blackbirds*, a series about a character named Miriam Black who gets vivid impressions of how and when a person will die by touching them (and then gets embroiled in a variety of crime plots).

> The man, the trucker, the Frankenstein. Louis. He is going to die in thirty days, at 7:25 pm. And it is going to be a horrible scene. Miriam sees a lot of death play out on the stage inside her skull. Blood and broken glass and dead eyes form the backdrop to her mind. But it's rare that she sees murder. Health problems, all the time. Car accidents and other personal disasters, over and over again. But murder. That is a rare bird.

Wendig uses sentence fragments for the moments that Miriam touches people and sees their death because the visions come to her in fractured images, missing context.

Here's another example from Irish author Sally Rooney's literary novel *Intermezzo,* about two brothers whose father has died and who are involved in socially complicated romantic relationships. Ivan is twenty-two and something of a chess prodigy, and Peter is an edgy lawyer ten years older. Peter's voice is notably clipped and terse, often relying on fragments.

> Clanking of a door somewhere inside now, and he turns, looks down the cool grey corridor. Walking towards him, dark hair piled up glossy on top of her head. Garda beside her. The lovely Naomi. Tear in her black tights, scraped knee, bleeding he can see a little. In her leather jacket, chewing gum. Lips he has how many times kissed. In fondness, frustration, irresistible desire.

Peter's syntax contrasts with the fuller and longer sentence structure of his younger brother, Ivan, a more emotional creature who still has the youthful naivete his brother appears to have lost:

> Thursday evening, Ivan is waiting for his brother in a dimly lit restaurant. Elsewhere he can see rich people eating expensive meals, and soon his brother will arrive, another rich person basically, and they will eat a meal together also. Why not? Peter, though overly motivated by the acquisition of personal wealth, Ivan thinks, and often obnoxious, and not as smart as he

thinks he is, nonetheless has talked sense about a couple of things down the years. At least on a few significant points, in fact, Peter has been right, and Ivan himself has been wrong.

One can speculate on what Rooney is trying to convey stylistically through the sentence structure. On the one hand, it helps to distinguish their voices; on the other, the fragmented voice reflects Peter's more jaded, less emotionally accessible nature, and the longer sentences, Ivan's youth.

Punctuation for Rhythm

Just as words have energy and texture, punctuation also contributes to sentence energy. Em dashes, commas, colons, semicolons, sentence fragments, and clipped sentences can create effects such as pauses and accelerations; they can even shape emotional nuance.

Em dashes, for instance, can suddenly—almost breathlessly—redirect the flow of a sentence. They can mimic interruption, urgency, or a quick aside that adds texture to voice. Colons can slow a sentence down, creating a deliberate pause that prepares the reader for something significant: a reveal, a punchline, or an insight that deserves emphasis.

Commas are subtler ways to suggest hesitation, anticipation, or accumulation. (And my work is, apparently, lousy with them. "Let your sentences breathe, Jordan," says my friend and editor, Levi.) They orchestrate pacing by offering a quick breath, making sure that words and ideas don't run together or get confused. On the other hand, commas can be used incorrectly in place of a necessary period, running sentences together when a pause is required.

Semicolons, on the other hand, can deliver an effect that's somewhere between the abruptness of a period and the softer pause of a comma; they provide connection and separation at once, and a lot of people struggle to use them. Most commonly, they're used when you want to join two independent but related sentences. They can also be used to divide items in a list, when within the list one or more of the items contains commas. The semicolons let readers know which items in the list are complete entities. Otherwise, a semicolon may have a harder stop than a comma.

Sometimes an author will also do away with punctuation for effect. For example, I love the way Henry Hoke embodies the voice of a mountain lion grappling with climate crisis, desire, and identity in his novel *Open Throat*. A mountain lion wouldn't naturally know punctuation or grammar ;-)

> a while ago I wouldn't fantasize about eating a person
>
> what the girls said makes sense
>
> I'm not sure what a scare city mentality is but I have it
>
> here is called different things by different people mostly they say ellay but they also say the park or Hollywood

Author Salley Rooney also tends to leave off quotation marks in dialogue in her novels. She used to use em dashes to signify a person speaking, but in a recent interview she gave in the magazine, *STET*,[7] she said, "I can't remember ever really using quotation marks—I don't see any need for them, and I don't understand the function they perform in a novel, marking off some particular pieces of the text as quotations. I mean, it's a novel written in the first person; isn't it all a quotation?"

She makes an interesting point!

Don't be afraid to play with word sounds and sentence rhythms repeatedly until you feel you've found the perfect formula. In fact, it reminds me of attending a reading by the writer ZZ Packer many years ago. As she read from her published book, she did so with a pencil in hand and would mark her book while she read. Asked about it by an audience member afterward, she said that every time she read her work aloud, she found something to refine. On that note, reading your work aloud is an excellent way to catch the kind of sentence-level things that our eyes easily glaze over.

This chapter contains a lot of suggestions, some more complex than others, for ways to work on your sentences. What matters most is that you consider them deeply and recognize that your words have impact well beyond simply conveying information.

In Summary

- **Sound shapes voice:** Play with the energies and frequencies of musicality, texture, and rhythm to create voice and tone.

- **Lyricism enriches voice:** Incorporating poetic techniques like imagery, metaphor, and simile adds depth, beauty, and thematic resonance to your sentences.

- **Dialect conveys identity:** Draw upon dialect to capture specific identities—place, culture, and time period—but avoid stereotypes and inaccuracies.

- **Alliteration creates rhythm and feeling:** Repeating consonant sounds can enhance sensory experience, establish mood, and reinforce emotional or energetic nuances within sentences.

- **Vowels and assonance carry emotional nuance:** Choosing specific vowel sounds can influence the mood, energy, and emotional texture of sentences.

- **Parallelism emphasizes ideas:** Using repeated grammatical structures can help create rhythm and momentum and highlight similarities and contrasts.

- **Repetition intensifies emotional impact:** Purposeful repetition of words or phrases can create rhythm, emphasize themes, and shape tone.

- **Sentence length and punctuation control pacing and mood:** Varied sentence length, intentional fragments, and strategic punctuation (commas, dashes, semicolons) significantly affect the rhythm, pace, and emotional resonance of writing, shaping the reader's experience.

- **Read your work aloud:** One of the best ways to revise at the sentence level is to hear your work aloud (if this is possible for you).

VOICE LESSONS

Writing Exercises

Now, you give it a try!

Lyricism and Imagery

Choose an ordinary object or a simple action (making coffee, tying shoelaces, washing dishes) and write a paragraph describing it as lyrically as possible.

- Use metaphors, similes, vivid imagery, and sensory details.
- Experiment with language that might enhance the emotion or deeper meaning behind this ordinary act.

Dialect Exploration

Write a short scene featuring dialogue in a dialect familiar to you.

- Pay attention to rhythm, vocabulary, and phrasing unique to this dialect.
- Read it aloud to see how the rhythm and authenticity come through.

- If a dialect isn't familiar, research or listen to authentic examples and attempt to capture the voice respectfully without stereotyping.

Alliteration Play

Write a paragraph using intentional alliteration to capture a mood, movement, or emotional intensity.

- Try crafting two versions: one subtle, one more intense.
- Read both versions aloud. Note how alliteration affects pacing, tone, and rhythm.

Parallelism Practice

Compose a passage (a paragraph or a short scene) employing parallel phrases, images, grammatical structures, or other sentence components.

- Use parallelism to build momentum, emphasize contrasts, or clarify meaning.
- Experiment by using parallel structures to show similarities or stark contrasts between characters, emotions, or ideas.

Word Sounds and Emotion

Choose two short scenes or descriptions to write, each aiming for a distinct mood (tense vs. peaceful).

- Deliberately select words based on their vowel / consonant sounds as discussed by Tsur (harsh vs. soft sounds, bright vs. dark vowels).
- Compare how each scene's word choices contribute to its emotional atmosphere.

Repetition (Anaphora / Epistrophe)

Write two short poetic prose pieces:

- First piece: Use anaphora, repeating a word or phrase at the beginning of sentences or clauses.
- Second piece: Use epistrophe, repeating a phrase or word at the end of sentences.
- Reflect on how each affects the rhythm, emotional intensity, and overall feeling of your prose.

Sentence-Length Variation

Write a single paragraph twice, once using primarily short sentences, then rewriting it using mostly longer sentences.

- Then, blend both to create a balanced mix.
- Notice how sentence length and cadence shape the tone, mood, pacing, and readability of your writing.

"The secret of being boring is to say everything."

—V̲oltaire

CHAPTER 11

Cutting Clutter

Refining Voice

If voice doesn't emerge right out of the gate for you, don't fret; voice can be refined. This doesn't mean that voices must *be refined*, as a quality judgment, but it may not fully take shape until you chip away at it. If you've determined that all the character and expressive elements we've discussed are working, it's likely something at the word or sentence level that's keeping your voice from radiating off the page the way you want. If Chapter 10 was about adding and shaping voice through linguistic and literary tricks, this chapter is about what you can cut and refine to let voice emerge as you intend.

While we'll discuss some rules, habits, or practices for refining your sentences and thus voice, once again I offer this caveat: There are millions of ways to write, the English language is not the god of languages, and most importantly, trust your instincts and style. For every "rule," there's a writer who breaks it so beautifully, readers couldn't care less, and for every convention that has been standardized, there is an original, true, or unique one that matters more to you.

Paying Attention to Your Sentences

Great stories and great characters can sometimes be undermined by bloated or saggy sentences that get in the way of their own clarity, that meander without direction, or that lean too heavily into literary devices.

At the same time, sometimes writers can use their sentences too serviceably, with no panache, forgetting to pay attention to their nuances, their flow, and their rhythm.

This chapter will discuss some of the things that clutter and hamper sentences and help you try to carve them away.

Unintended Repetition

Repetition is a linguistic tool that can create rhythm, as you saw in Chapter 10, but it can also crowd a sentence when it's overused or abused. When you use the same word, or a similar word more than once within a sentence or a paragraph without conscious style, it often stands out to the reader and interrupts the flow if you didn't intend it.

Example: The rain started to fall harder and harder, and soon the streets were flooded with water. The water was rising quickly, and I knew we had to leave before it got worse.

Revised: A drizzle became a pour, flooding the streets. The banks of the river rose so quickly, we had to flee before it got worse.

In the revision, we get rid of the repetition of "water" but also tighten and improve upon the descriptions of rain "falling harder", get rid of the filter phrase "I knew", and replace "leave" with "flee", which conjures more urgency.

Redundancy

A related concept, redundancy, is when you repeat something but in a different way, encumbering a sentence by slowing its pace and clarity or diluting its impact. Readers are quick to pick up on unnecessary (and unintended) repetition, which makes the prose feel less polished. Redundancies are words and phrases you can eliminate without changing the significance of the passage.

It can be subtle, suggests Theodore A. Rees Cheney in his book *Getting the Words Right*. For example: "He was popular with the people." Popular assumes "with the people" so you don't need to say it.

Or it can be more overt, like: "He kicked the door of his closet because he was mad. 'I'm so angry,' he shouted."

In the latter example, the action, the thought, and the dialogue all communicate the same thing. Pick one, or maybe two.

To catch redundancies, it can help to read your work aloud. Additionally, you can ask: Does this word / phrase add new information? If not, cut it. Lastly, trust your reader. Readers can infer meaning from context, so avoid overexplaining.

Cut to the Chase

It's easy in the drafting phase of writing to encumber sentences with more words than are necessary. Sometimes these are words that don't add energy or clarity to a sentence, or like above, when you explain too much to the reader. These can be cut or revised.

> *Example*: The storm had been raging for a long time, and the wind was blowing very hard. The trees were swaying and creaking, making me feel like they were about to fall over. It was so loud and intense, I couldn't think clearly.
>
> *Revised*: The storm raged and howled, the trees swaying so much, I feared they'd fall. The roar of wind and rain pelting my windows drowned my thoughts.

Too Many Sentences

Sometimes you're trying to explain or describe a thing with more sentences than you need.

Example: The library stood at the end of a long, winding path. There were tall oak trees lining both sides of the path, and their branches created a canopy overhead. The entrance to the library was marked by a large wooden door with intricate carvings.

Revised: The library stood at the end of a winding path, flanked by a canopy of leafy oaks. A carved wooden door marked the entrance.

Weak Filler Words

Filler words can creep into writing, adding bulk without substance. They often make sentences longer and less direct, diluting their impact. Let's look at some of these.

- There is / was / are

Example: There was a man with a scary expression walking up my steps.

Revised: A grimacing man stomped up my steps.

- It was

Example: It was the moment that changed everything.

Revised: That moment changed everything.

- the fact that

Example: The fact that she was late frustrated me.

Revised: Her lateness frustrated me.

- in order to (usually "to" alone is enough—though there are times I prefer the rhythm of "in order to" over "to")

Example: She studied in order to pass the test.

Revised: She studied to pass the test.

- start to / begin to (Often, the action itself is enough)

Example: He started to run toward me.

Revised: He ran toward me.

Vague Words

In a related vein, some words offer so little clarity that their vagueness takes away from your message.

- appears to

Example: The man grasped his throat, turned red, and appeared to be choking. (Is he choking or isn't he?)

Revised: The man grasped his throat and turned red. "He's choking!" I shouted.

- kind of / sort of / a little bit

Example: She was kind of annoyed. (Is she annoyed

or not?)

Revised: She was annoyed.

- really / very / quite (Often unnecessary and can be replaced with stronger adjectives)

Example: The house was really big.

Revised: The house was enormous.

- somewhat / somehow / in some way

Example: He was somewhat distracted.

Revised: He was distracted.

- almost / practically / virtually

Example: She was practically crying.

Revised She was on the verge of tears.

- basically / essentially / generally

Example: Basically, the plan was to meet at noon.

Revised: The plan was to meet at noon.

Excessive Modifiers

I love a good adjective and adverb. You won't hear me telling you not to use them. However, I do recommend using them sparingly; too many modifiers can clutter sentences. Let's look at an over-the-top example of modifier madness. Notice your experience when reading it. (If the phrase "purple prose" comes to mind, you're not wrong.)

> *Example*: The crisp, bone-chilling night air whistled eerily through the dense, towering pine trees, sending a shuddering, uneasy feeling down Jason's already tense, stiff spine. The nearly full, slightly hazy moon cast a faint, silvery glow over the damp, uneven forest floor, where tangled, gnarled roots twisted menacingly like grasping, skeletal fingers. With each slow, cautious step, his worn, mud-caked boots crunched softly against the brittle, frost-dusted leaves, the only sound in the otherwise silent, ghostly, desolate wilderness.

What could we edit out of this to make it tighter?

> *Revised:* The cold night air whistled through the pine trees, and Jason shivered. The moon cast a pale glow over the forest floor, just enough to see the tangled roots jutting out like grasping fingers. With each careful step, his boots crunched against frosty leaves, the only sound.

Clichés

Clichés are overused phrases that lose freshness and specificity, those essential voice qualities. Clichés often fail precisely because they are so generic and lack the emotion or action you want to convey. That said, some characters intentionally speak in clichés, so if that's the case, don't feel as if you must root them all out.

Some clichés you may be familiar with:

- The calm before the storm
- All that glitters is not gold
- Between a rock and a hard place
- Think outside the box
- Every cloud has a silver lining
- It's a blessing in disguise
- Fresh as a daisy

Your characters and narrator have a unique way of seeing things. Take "fresh as a daisy." A character who lives in the desert may not think of anything resembling daisies when they think fresh. Perhaps, to them, *fresh* equals clean water and ocean air.

Consider your character's unique, personal, and individual take on that particular item, object, feeling, or state of mind, and rewrite clichés.

Filter Words

Filter words put distance between the reader and the character's experience. John Gardner writes in *The Art of Fiction: Notes on Craft for Young Writers* that, "Generally speaking—though no laws are absolute in fiction—vividness urges that almost every occurrence of such phrases as 'she noticed' and 'she saw' be suppressed in favor of direct presentation of the thing seen."

He also describes the filters as "some observing consciousness" that is not the character. There are different kinds of filters to consider:

Sensory: *saw, tasted, smelled, felt, heard, sensed, etc.*

- He smelled the rich brine of chicken broth bubbling.
- She heard a cacophony of birds.
- They saw a giant wave approaching.

If you remove the filter in each of these, you can cut straight to the sensation instead. For example: "The rich brine of chicken broth hit his nose as he entered the house." Now, we're *in* the sensory experience.

Intellectual: *knew, understood, perceived, learned, wondered, decided, considered, noticed, realized, etc.*

- He realized he was feeling angry

- She considered whether this was the right time to confront him.

- They were surprised to notice how late it had grown

What do we do when we realize we are angry? Perhaps, "His fists clenched at the thought of her." Maybe instead of the characters noticing the time, they discover that it's now dark when before it was light.

Emotional: *yearned, wanted, dreamed, loved, ached, enjoyed, etc.*

- She reflected on the pain of his rejection.

- He understood that she did not intend to hurt him.

- They knew it was time to tell the truth.

What does "the pain of his rejection" feel like? What other way could this be expressed? *How* did he understand she did not intend to hurt him? What cues tell them it's time to tell the truth? Rewriting to omit the filters often wakes prose up and fleshes out meaning.

Melodrama / Overwrought Prose

Writers often ask, when does prose become over the top or melodramatic—a term often known as "purple." It varies, but a few instances are:

- When there is too much going on in a sentence (not concise, too many gerunds, clunky syntax)

- When the descriptions don't match the content of the scene (too many modifiers)

- When there's excess emotional content (characters over-emoting)

- When the writer is relying on telling versus showing (explaining too much)

You might be familiar with the Bulwer-Lytton contest, in which writers compete to write the worst first sentence for a novel? Let's dissect one of the winners:

> The sun oozed over the horizon, shoved aside darkness, crept along the greensward, and, with sickly fingers, pushed through the castle window, revealing the pillaged princess, hand at throat, crown asunder, gaping in frenzied horror at the sated, sodden amphibian lying beside her, disbelieving the magnitude of the frog's deception, screaming madly, "You lied!"

While the sentence is a lot of fun at face value, and writing badly is the whole point, what exactly makes it "bad"?

- It's one really long sentence.

- It's packed with adjectives and descriptors that tell rather than show.

- The choice of adjectives feels melodramatic, such as "frenzied horror" and "screaming madly."

- It telegraphs, which is to say, it tells us something in a passive narrative way about the frog's deception before she says, "You lied." The dialogue would suffice.

Prose Without Style

On the other side of purple prose is prose that has no sense of style or rhythm whatsoever. It lacks any real descriptors, character energy, or voice details, and could beg to be fleshed out.

> *Example*: It's night now. The stars are out. She'd better go to sleep. She has a busy day tomorrow. She can't be tired.

In this example, the sentence lengths don't vary. There's no emotion or internal reflection. These are just serviceable sentences. What could you add to give it some voice?

Revision can be a way of cutting away all that is not essential to your character's voice, paring down, and sometimes plumping back up.

I like to think of revising for voice as being a lot like the sculptor carving away the excess clay to reveal their true creation beneath. Cutting clutter doesn't mean stripping your writing of what makes it unique; if anything, it amplifies voice by getting rid of obscuring elements. The key is to revise with intention and with your character or narrator in mind.

In Summary

- **Voice emerges through refining:** While voice may not fully emerge at first, refining and trimming your sentences can help bring it to life. Pay attention to the word or sentence level to enhance clarity, rhythm, and emotion.

- **Remove unintended repetition:** Repetition, when used unconsciously, can clutter a sentence and interrupt the flow.

- **Remove redundancy:** Redundancy occurs when phrases restate the same idea, adding length without value. Cut for clarity.

- **Cut to the chase:** Cut or streamline overexplaining and weak filler words that lengthen sentences without adding substance.

- **Avoid the vague:** Cut that which lacks specificity to create more vivid, precise writing.

- **Cut excessive modifiers:** Pare adjectives and adverbs that clutter sentences and dilute their impact.

- **Scale back the melodrama:** Strive for balance in your emotional descriptions.

VOICE LESSONS

Writing Exercises

Now, you give it a try!

Refining Sentence Structure

Take a passage you've recently written (or select one at random) and focus on refining it for voice and rhythm. Look for places where the sentence structure can be varied to create a more dynamic flow.

- Identify sentences that feel stiff or mechanical.

- Experiment with varying the length of sentences. Combine short sentences for impact or break up long sentences to prevent them from feeling like a run-on.

- Eliminate weak filler words and phrases (like "there is," "it was," "began to," etc.) and replace them with stronger, more direct verbs or phrases.

- Add or adjust descriptive details to enhance the emotional or visual appeal of the writing. Aim for precise word choices that contribute to the overall tone.

Cutting Unnecessary Words

Choose a passage from your work (it could be from a longer scene or a paragraph you find overly detailed). Your goal is to cut words or phrases that don't add to the meaning, mood, or clarity of the scene.

- Highlight weak filler words, redundancy, and vague terms.
- Eliminate these without losing the essence of what you're trying to convey.
- After cutting, read the passage aloud to ensure it still flows naturally and makes sense.

Simplifying Melodrama or Overwrought Prose

Take a melodramatic or overly emotional passage from your writing and revise it to remove excess adjectives, adverbs, and over-the-top descriptions. Focus on simplifying the prose to make it clearer without losing emotional impact or the essence of your voice.

- Identify the most exaggerated or overly emotional aspects of your passage.

- Remove or replace melodramatic descriptors with simpler, more subtle language.
- Add specific actions or dialogue that show emotion without telling the reader directly.
- Aim for an evocative, grounded scene that allows the reader to feel the emotion without being overwhelmed by it.

Transforming Clichés

Pick two to three clichés from this list (or pull from an easy internet search) and rewrite them from your character's or narrator's POV and voice to have the same approximate meaning. Try not to replace one cliché with another. The goal is to say something in a "new" way that reflects the character's or narrator's unique way of seeing the world, of speaking, and so on.

- The calm before the storm
- All that glitters is not gold
- Between a rock and a hard place
- Think outside the box
- Every cloud has a silver lining
- It's a blessing in disguise
- Fresh as a daisy

PART THREE

Tone

> *"A writer doesn't have a soundtrack or a strobe light to build the effect she wants. She has conflict, surprise, imagery, details, the words she chooses, and the way she arranges them in sentences."*
>
> —Adair Lara, *Naked, Drunk, and Writing*

CHAPTER 12

Tone Evokes a Feeling or Mood

What Is Tone?

While voice emerges from a character's history, personality, and manner of expression and is shaped by their syntax and lexicon, tone can be considered a feeling, mood, or attitude that the voice delivers or conveys. As much as I've separated out voice and tone into discrete sections, it's important to note that voice and tone are often indelibly intertwined. A character's voice may be *inherently* broody, plaintive, or wry, thus driving the tone of the story as a whole or even a given scene.

However, as Matthew Salesses writes in *Craft in the Real World*, "Tone should not be mistaken for the *protagonist's* orientation toward the world, however, even for a first-person narrator. The protagonist might find the world to be a wonderful place, but the book might contradict her."

Some genres have *expected* tones—a mystery might be serious, a thriller intense and edgy, a rom-com funny and lighthearted. Yet as we saw in Chapter 9 on genre, when you have genre crossover, you sometimes have tone crossover too. Hence, there are humorous thrillers and sexy fantasy stories, to name a couple.

In memoir and essay, it's not uncommon to find people who've lived through traumas expressing gallows humor or even recounting pain in a detached manner, as though the experiences happened to someone else. That's one of the beautiful things about writing a true story such as memoir or essay: You get to *choose* the tone, curating your own life as you wish to present it.

Often, you don't even think about tone until you receive critique that the tone is off or doesn't match the content. While it's helpful if you know the tone you want to set in your story from the beginning, not everyone does until you've written the story. One way to get started is to ask yourself what mood, feeling, or attitude you want the reader to take away from their read.

With tone, remember, the goal is to evoke a feeling or mood in the reader, or as Donald Hall and Sven Birkerts say in *Writing Well*, "[T]one is the writer's choice of a connection with the reader." Salesses describes it as "an orientation toward the world." You may be able to identify tone in your own work by asking how you want to make the reader feel.

In a previous chapter, we looked at a passage from Rene Denfeld's novel *The Enchanted* and I want to look at it again through the lens of tone. One of the things I love so much about her book is that the tone feels intentionally innocent, almost magical, for a novel that is about very difficult topics. Let's look at the passage again, and as you read it (again, with certain details elided), consider where you think this story is set. What place is this narrator describing? How does it make you feel?

> This is an enchanted place. Others don't see it but I do. I see every cinder block, every hallway and doorway. I see the doorways that lead to the secret stairs and the stairs that take you into stone towers and the towers that take you to windows…I see the soft-tufted night birds as they drop from the heavens. I see the golden horses as they run deep under the earth, heat flowing like molten metal from their backs …

When I ask students where they think this is set, they tell me things like "a castle" or "a fantasy setting." The narrator's tone is reverent and delighted, and magical, indeed. But the setting is actually death row in an old stone prison. This novel seeks to pry us free from our biases and expectations to explore the nuances of human behavior. Thus, we get a magical tone for a novel about a woman whose job it is to help men get off death row, but it's about more than that; it's about the systems that put people in prison, about the traumas that drive crimes, about the insidious nature of corruption, and more. I've thought a lot about how she could have written the novel with a gritty or hard-edged tone, but by giving us this softer tone, it allows us to enter material that could otherwise be hard to digest or into which we might bring judgments or stereotypes.

Now let's look at an excerpt with a vastly different tone, from Alissa Nutting's wild novel *Made for Love* (which was adapted into a TV show for HBO Max). A little scene setting here: The main character, Hazel Green, has fled the compound of her billionaire husband, Byron, who runs a tech empire (clearly modeled after an Elon Musk / Mark Zuckerberg template). She freaked out after he made clear his intent to implant a microchip in both of their brains that will allow them to know each other's every thought (with or without her consent). This section is a flashback she's having of the night he introduced the idea.

> Suddenly the moon was wide and full above her head like a spotlight. The flamingo, with its raised, tucked-under plastic leg suggested the shape of Byron kneeling down on one knee, and memory flooded her. This was how he'd presented her with the microchip that he wanted to place in her brain: Byron had cleverly, in a faux-romantic overture, put the chip inside a velvet ring box, gotten down on one knee, opened up the box's lid and said, Hazel Green, will you meld with me?

TONE EVOKES A FEELING OR MOOD

What is the tone? A few things stand out to me in this passage that evoke its tone. First, note that instead of a full moon being beautiful, it feels like a "spotlight"—which I associate with something glaring and too bright. She's comparing her *husband* to a fake plastic flamingo. The scene evokes something romantic, with a velvet ring box, and him dropping to one knee, yet it completely upends romance; rather than a marriage proposal, he asks her if she'll "meld" with him, and what he means is meld their minds through this bizarre technology. It's humor but absurdist humor. It's humor as social commentary. It's supposed to make you laugh but also ask *hmmm, how do I feel about that*? We'll look at a different humorous tone in another example later to show how humor can come in a variety of tones.

Meanwhile, what is the tone of this passage from *Long Bright River* by Liz Moore?

> There's a body on the Gurney Street tracks. Female, age unclear, probably overdose, says the dispatcher.
>
> *Kacey*, I think. This is a twitch, a reflex, something sharp and subconscious that lives inside me and sends the same message racing to the same base part of my brain every time a female is reported.

This happens to be the opening paragraph of the novel, so it's our first introduction to the character's voice and tone. Notice the factually reported nature of the first two sentences. No emotion, no reaction, just details reporting a deceased woman. It wouldn't take much sleuthing to determine this is a crime novel of some kind, maybe mystery, maybe thriller. We can probably gather that this person is a first responder or a law enforcement officer. The tone shifts, however, when the character has a single thought, a name: "Kacey." Here we feel the tiniest bit of emotion in that "something sharp and subconscious" that "sends a message racing to the same base part of my brain..." The tone is not lighthearted, and it's not funny. Whether you want to call this heavy or moody or intense, we understand that this is a serious story, in which the narrator has a personal investment that informs her work.

Lastly, let's look at a final tone example from Andrew Sean Greer's Pulitzer Prize winning novel, *Less*, about a writer named Arthur Less who travels the world on a literary tour while dealing with heartbreak. In this scene, he is guest teaching in Germany, where he doesn't speak German very well.

> "I am your Mr. Professor."

> He is not. Unaware of the enormous difference between the German Professor and Dozent, the former being a rank achieved only through decades of internment in the academic prison, the latter a mere parolee, Less has given himself a promotion.

> "And now, I am sorry, I must kill most of you."

TONE EVOKES A FEELING OR MOOD

With this startling announcement, he proceeds to weed out any students who are not registered in the Global Linguistics and Literature Department."

The tone is humorous, but it's different from the absurdist *Made for Love* humor, and it's also not slapstick humor. What makes it funny? Keep in mind that this is an omniscient POV as well, so the narrator is *observing* Less and then telling the reader, almost as though we are in on a special aside with the narrator *about* Less. Humor emerges from the fact that Less is a writer and a teacher but doesn't speak the language he's teaching in well enough to get some key nuances correct. He launches into his introduction by calling himself "your Mr. Professor" which is charmingly funny all on its own, but more so when we learn that he's actually given himself "a promotion" because he should have called himself a "dozent."

Furthermore, he can't even accurately say he's dropping students from class in German—he announces he will have to "kill" most of them.

It's funny in an arch way—that is, where the humor is making fun of something. In this case, the tone is like a wink at how seriously academia takes itself, missing the forest for the trees.

What Creates Tone?

Now that we've had an overview of tone, what actually creates tone at the word or sentence level? What makes those passages different from one another? Let's take a closer look at the same passages. Sometimes the genre dictates word choices and sentence structure—a hard-boiled detective novel may not have lyrical long sentences. A humorous novel may rely upon short, punchy sentences or funny juxtapositions. Sometimes it's character personality or context.

The Enchanted: *Lyrical sentence techniques*

> This is an enchanted place. Others don't see it but I do. I see every cinder block, every hallway and doorway. I see the doorways that lead to the secret stairs and the stairs that take you into stone towers and the towers that take you to windows…I see the soft-tufted night birds as they drop from the heavens. I see the golden horses as they run deep under the earth, heat flowing like molten metal from their backs…

There's a poetic, rhythmic structure to this character's description of the prison that might be part of what makes us feel like it's fantasy or something otherworldly. Some of the sentences have the rhythm of run-ons. He sounds as though he is almost singing or humming the phrases, with their conscious repetition of the words "doorway" and "stairs" and "towers" and the poetic imagery of "golden horses" with "molten metal" flowing from their backs.

TONE EVOKES A FEELING OR MOOD

Made for Love: *Juxtaposition in imagery*

> Suddenly the moon was wide and full above her head like a spotlight. The flamingo, with its raised, tucked-under plastic leg suggested the shape of Byron kneeling down on one knee, and memory flooded her. This was how he'd presented her with the microchip that he wanted to place in her brain: Byron had cleverly, in a faux-romantic overture, put the chip inside a velvet ring box, gotten down on one knee, opened up the box's lid and said, Hazel Green, will you meld with me?

The tone in this passage is created almost entirely by the juxtaposition of imagery. The setup is romance, but the delivery is comedy. The full moon becomes a spotlight, a beloved on bended knee becomes a plastic flamingo, a velvet ring box offers not a profession of marriage but of mind melding. It's funny, but in a kind of "Who does that?" sort of way. Once again, it functions as social commentary, given that a certain billionaire in the real world has begun testing brain chips.

Long Bright River: *Dispassionate language*

> There's a body on the Gurney Street tracks. Female, age unclear, probably overdose, says the dispatcher.
>
> *Kacey*, I think. This is a twitch, a reflex, something sharp and subconscious that lives inside me and sends the same message racing to the same base part of my brain every time a female is reported.

In this passage it's hard to miss the dispassionate language: *body, female, overdose, dispatcher*. Once again, we note there's very little emotional language or imagery except for "a twitch, a reflex". That barely registers as an emotion; in fact, it's more like a chemical signal in her brain, as though this character can't even let herself *have* a feeling. The word choices and the lack of emotional content create the tone.

Less: *Contradictions and commentary*

"I am your Mr. Professor."

> He is not. Unaware of the enormous difference between the German Professor and Dozent, the former being a rank achieved only through decades of internment in the academic prison, the latter a mere parolee, Less has given himself a promotion.

"And now, I am sorry, I must kill most of you."

> With this startling announcement, he proceeds to weed out any students who are not registered in the Global Linguistics and Literature Department.

There's an aspect of meta-fiction at work here in *Less* (a kind of self-conscious allusion or mocking of the artificiality or literary convention of the work itself). The voice takes an academic tone, in phrases like "decades of internment in the academic prison" and "mere parolee" but is *making fun* of academia at the same time. Moreover, the use of the omniscient voice to "correct" Less for his imperfect German comes across as funny, because it's evident that Less is taking himself quite seriously at that moment.

Lastly, it should be said that tone can be tricky for some people. That is, both writer and reader ascribe meaning to certain words and phrases, and thus while one tone may be intended, it may not translate 100%. If you've ever tried having a discussion by text message that turned into an argument, you surely know what I mean. A lot of tone may be dependent on context as well, and sometimes tones do shift over the course of a story, or from scene to scene. Sometimes you just need to rely on feedback to get it right.

Tone in Memoir and Essay

Though many of the choices that create tone are the same in memoir and essay as in fiction, there are some differences based upon the fact the narrator is almost always you, as we discussed in Chapter 6.

I want to revisit the idea that memoir and essay give writers the freedom to curate a unique voice and tone—one that reflects their personal identity, version of events, or self-reflection. In this way, many memoirists and essayists place tone at the center of their work, using it to reclaim or reframe the experiences that have shaped them.

With memoir and essay, however, there are fewer conceits of fiction—the reader *knows* the writer is also the one to whom the things in your story have happened, so there's a lot more direct intimacy.

So, let's look at how some memoir and essay writers handle tone in their works. I'll begin with a book of essays I adore called *Pain Woman Takes Your Keys, and Other Essays from a Nervous System* by Sonya Huber, about the onset of, and later living with, chronic illness. The essays range from straightforward to poetic, and she continually plays with imagery and personification of her pain as she grapples with it.

> The pain creature that overlaps with my body is born anew each day, a colorful double image superimposed with shimmering edges. She and I are strung together with the most delicate meniscus of surface tension, the membrane of an amoeba constantly evolving. She nibbles at my edges, though I try to hold her in check with the wavelike motion of my cilia, the silver line of to-do list tension that keeps me afloat and a step ahead. But I can't stay ahead of my pain-sister, and she enfolds me in the salt water of my origins, unable to stop the storm surge of ocean where we evolved together. We wanted to be sentient. We wanted to feel. And this is the cost of our evolved nervous system.

The tone here is reminiscent of Rene Denfeld's *The Enchanted* in that it offers something potentially difficult to describe and literally painful, which could be presented in a negative light. Yet by giving her pain an identity—turning it into a creature, a "pain-sister" that is both of her but separate, the tone is curious, concerned, almost scholarly. I find it makes it easier to access, whether that is her intent or not.

Now let's contrast that tone with one in which emotional pain is evoked quite potently, but in a very different way. From Emily Rapp Black's memoir *Sanctuary*, in which she explores the idea of resilience after loss, several years after losing her young son, Ronan, to Tay-Sachs disease.

> Content note: Suicidal feelings

> Peering into the cavernous gorge was like encountering the impact of long-ago violence, perhaps a prehistoric stomp from the gigantic foot of an angry, mythical animal on a murderous cross-country trek. Feeling like a witness to some great destruction appealed to me. I stretched my arms farther and let them dangle, helped by gravity, until my fingertips began to tingle, and until the noise and chatter of people walking past began to dissipate and then disappear. I was lost in the promise of this emptiness, the sound of it, which was the absence of sound apart from a small rock loosening from the steep bank to tumble into the dry brush, rolling down down down until it disappeared from view. I closed my eyes and heard *whomp whomp whomp* like an invitation: *Yes. Jump. Do it*. The space was hollow, magnetic, literally an opening. A mouth to fall into, as deep as any desire.

The pain of losing a child is immense, monumental, and Rapp Black does not shy away from a grief-stricken tone. What impressed me, though, is how she captures and expresses her grief through her use of metaphor and simile—as a "long-ago violence" and a "mythical animal on a murderous cross-country trek." The gorge itself is also a metaphor for her grief—something so enormous, it can never be filled, and which beckons to her to be lost in its depths forever.

Next, in Ariel Henley's memoir *A Face for Picasso*, she tells the story of growing up with Crouzon syndrome, a rare condition that causes the bones in an infant's head to fuse prematurely. She and her twin sister, Zan, underwent dozens of intense medical procedures that changed their faces over the years. Let's look at the tone of the opening pages.

> I am ugly. There's a mathematical equation to prove it. Or so I was told by the boy who sat behind me the first day of seventh-grade art class.
>
> I'm going to stick my pencil through the back of your eye," he told me, laughing. It's not like you could get much uglier. Even the teacher thinks so."
>
> He continued poking me in the shoulder with his pencil, but I said nothing.
>
> At twelve years old, I was already used to people identifying my flaws and commenting on my ugliness. It comes with the territory of being born with a facial difference as a result of Crouzon syndrome—a rare craniofacial disorder where the bones in the head fuse prematurely. My eyes were too far apart and too crooked, my nose too big.
>
> My jaw was too far back, my ears too low. There were regular appointments with doctors and surgeons trying to fix my twin sister, Zan, who was also born with the condition. Some of it was for medical purposes, other times for aesthetics.

If you notice less emotional weight in the words she chooses to describe a painful or humiliating experience in school, you're right. Henley is a master of delivering her story with measured dispassion. It's the kind of distance that only comes after a lifetime of having to deal with pain, ridicule, and assaults to her very identity as her face changes through surgeries. It's a tone that says: *You can try me, but I've heard it all. I'm not so easy to rile.* It doesn't mean she is empty of emotion. No, she is choosing to share with the reader the side or version of herself that refuses to be fazed by hateful words or cruel judgments.

Let's finish by looking at an example from Samantha Irby's book of essays *We Are Never Meeting in Real Life*, written almost as a series of conversations she's having with friends or monologues she might deliver live. It's in-your-face, irreverent, sometimes slapstick. Here's an example from one essay titled "A Bomb Probably."

> Everyone I know is having a goddamned baby and what that means is you can't just stop by your homegirl's house unannounced with a bottle of Carménère and a couple of tubes of Pringles to watch hours of makeup tutorial videos on YouTube anymore. Because that baby might be sleeping or eating or doing its taxes, and you are going to mess it all up with your loud, single-person bullshit.

This tone is not begging you to take it too seriously. It's not going deep. It purports to be annoyed, but there's a hint of amusement within it. The tone is also self-aware; Irby knows she's being a little unreasonable but that's part of what makes it funny. It's also a setup, because in the next paragraph she reveals, "I am in a relationship now with a woman who has children, and let me just say that most certainly was *not* how I was expecting my destiny to knit itself together."

If tone isn't obvious to you right away, remember that it might be easier to identify upon revision, when you can see the fullness of your writing and gauge the tonal shifts. Most importantly, think about the emotions or attitudes you might want to leave your readers with when they put down your work.

In Summary

- **Voice versus tone:** Voice emerges from a character's history, personality, and manner of expression, while tone conveys a mood or feeling, though both work together.

- **Tone reflects mood and feelings:** Tone is the character's or narrator's emotional or mental attitude conveyed in the story and is influenced by the voice and the events unfolding.

- **Genres influence expected tone:** Different genres come with expected tones, but these can cross over in genres that blend elements.

- **Tone in memoir and essay:** In memoir and essays, writers have more control over tone to reflect their personal experiences and identity, allowing them to curate the feeling or perspective they want to express.

- **Tone can shift:** The tone in a piece of writing can shift throughout the narrative, influenced by character growth and the context of different scenes.

- **Tone is created through word choice and structure:** Sentence structure, word choice, and imagery all contribute to tone.

VOICE LESSONS

Writing Exercises

Now, you give it a try!

Tone Shift

Write a short scene in which a character must ask for something, using a clear tone, such as humorous or sad. Then, rewrite the same scene in a totally different tone. Focus on how changing word choice, sentence structure, imagery, and / or pacing shifts the emotional impact of the scene.

Voice vs. Tone Character Monologue

Write a monologue in which a character or narrator is describing a challenging personal experience. First, write the monologue in a neutral tone (neither too emotional nor too distant). Then rewrite it, adjusting the tone to be either extremely emotional (such as angry or overjoyed) or completely detached.

Genre and Tone Exercise

Pick a familiar story or fairy tale (*Little Red Riding Hood, Cinderella*). Write the opening of this story in three different genres: one as a horror story, one as a comedy, and one as a romance. Each version should maintain the original voice of the characters, but the tone should shift to reflect the genre's conventions.

"Watch your thoughts, they become your words; watch your words, they become your actions; watch your actions, they become your habits; watch your habits, they become your character; watch your character, it becomes your destiny."

— Lao Tzu

CHAPTER 13

Tone in Dialogue and Thoughts

Create Tone Through Dialogue and Thoughts

Though we touched upon both dialogue and thought cues as they lead to shaping voice in Chapter 3, let's look at them both again through the lens of tone. Dialogue is also often the easiest way to access voice, because we can truly "hear" our characters in our heads. For memoir and essay writers, it might be easy to recapture a moment in time by remembering a dialogue exchange.

Dialogue is often seen as the public-facing side of a character's voice—the aspect that others witness and hear. Thoughts, on the other hand, represent the more private side of voice. While they can have the same energy and movement as dialogue, they remain internal, unspoken.

Because of this, the tone of a character's thoughts can differ from the tone of their speech, especially when they're holding back from speaking, or omitting, certain feelings that exist primarily in their thoughts.

We'll look at some of the ways that tone translates in dialogue first, and then thoughts.

Tone in Dialogue

Author Jessica Page Morrell points out in her book *Between the Lines: Master the Subtle Elements of Fiction Writing* that not only is dialogue the speech that your characters exchange (which can also take the form of American Sign Language, telekinetic speaking in fantasy, and so on), it's "conversation's greatest hits."

In other words, dialogue is most effective when it's strategic and stylistic. Readers tend to get bored by dialogue that stays too long in mundane pleasantries. Though there's a time and a place for logistics and other minutiae, dialogue is a tool of character, scene, and plot development. What dialogue does best is reveal character's feelings, history, and goals, and dynamics between characters.

It's also a great place to reveal tone, since tone, emotion, and expression are all so closely tied together.

As discussed in Chapter 1, a character's voice is shaped in great part by their backstory. Thus, dialogue can be a great place to reveal some of those details, letting the tone communicate attitudes and opinions shaped by their past experiences or circumstances.

Let's look at a few examples of tone manifest in dialogue. The first comes from Melissa Febos's memoir about love and loss in essays, *Abandon Me*.

> *You are so beautiful,* she said again and again. *Your mouth, your mouth reinvents the word "mouth."*
>
> I squirmed under this scrutiny, laughed, but she stayed serious.
>
> *Your hips,* she said, pressing her mouth against them. *I didn't know what hips were before yours.*
>
> *Yeah, right,* I murmured, burying my fingers in her hair.
>
> *I mean it,* she said. *Touching you makes me feel like I have a hundred hands, makes me wish I had a hundred more.*

I don't think I need to clarify what's happening in this scene; the tone of the dialogue (here represented in italics) is clearly erotic but tender, not salacious. The use of hyperbole in "your mouth reinvents the word 'mouth'" and "I didn't know what hips were before yours" conveys a sense of adoration for the narrator that sounds like new love. There's a reverent tone of care and concern evident between the characters. There's also a tonal subtext that the narrator is a little uncomfortable with all this attention in the response, "yeah right" and "I squirmed under this scrutiny," but overall, we get the sense that the tone is one of mutual desire.

Now, here's another example with a very different tone, from Megan Abbott's psychological thriller, *Give Me Your Hand*. In it, protagonist Kit and her childhood best friend Diane haven't seen each other since they were teens, when they had falling out because of a dark confession Diane made. Now, decades later, they're going to be working together very closely as scientists, with Diane acting as Kit's boss on a research project. What tone does Diane's dialogue create? How does Kit seem to respond to it?

> "Diane," I start but I have nowhere to go, a sudden flapping in my chest.
>
> "Is there something," she says, turning to face me now, "you want to talk about?"
>
> Once she's called me on it, I can't think what to say.
>
> "There is so much to talk about," she continues, lowering her tinted goggles to her neck, looking at me. Her voice is stronger than I anticipated and forthright. "Seeing you here, I keep thinking about fate."
>
> "What?" I say, thinking I've misheard. "What did you say—"
>
> "There's so much between us," she says, softening her voice to a whisper. "The things we shared." She places her hand on my forearm. "My best friend."

Because the reader has the context that Diane once made a terrifying confession to Kit, all their dialogue interactions are filtered through that lens. Though Diane's words seem sweet on the surface, there's a threatening undertone, at least to Kit's way of thinking. Diane feels dangerous and the tone bears that out.

Here's one more from one of my favorite literary novels ever, *How to Tell Toledo from the Night Sky* by Lydia Netzer. In this scene, the co-protagonists, Irene and George, are astronomers drawn to each other but skirting the edges of their attraction. They attend a lecture that is so bad, they're both trying hard not to laugh during most of it. After, they engage in this dialogue:

> After it was over, she snapped her laptop shut and said, "Well, Dr. Dermont, thanks to you my notes for today consist of the word 'crap.' And here I thought you would only impede my work if I dated you."
>
> "You could have taken notes," he said. He stood up.
>
> "That's true," she said, relenting. "And anyway, I probably wouldn't have taken notes. Most of that lecture is in his published work, if you piece it together. If you take the spirit of the thing," Irene said.
>
> "I thought we weren't supposed to take the spirit of the thing. I thought we were to single the spirit into a blackened pile of ash and then count every molecule in the pile and call that the answer," George said.
>
> "George, you're a dreamer, I'm afraid," she said, throwing her laptop bag over her shoulder and letting him out of the row of seats. She gave him a smile.

While there is subtle flirtation happening between the two, unlike in the Febos example above, they haven't openly admitted their attraction. The tone feels a little adversarial, with Irene chastising George for being "bad" for her studies. Sarcasm often hides more tender feelings, and the reader senses that she likes him but is struggling to admit it. It's tense, for sure, but the tone isn't truly argumentative; it's wry, nudging us to understand that this attraction is being poorly denied.

Tonal Shifts in Dialogue

While a character's or narrator's voice may have a consistent tone throughout your book, tone *can* change in dialogue from scene to scene or even within a scene.

A character could start out conveying a silly, lighthearted tone in dialogue that is really covering up a feeling of humiliation or anger, or any other variation of tone. In code-switching moments, a character might suppress truer, more potent, even angry or hurt feelings in favor of a more context-acceptable tone, which can take an emotional toll.

In Julia May Jonas's darkly comic novel *Vladimir*, the protagonist, a popular English professor and writer, is dealing with an investigation of her husband engaging in inappropriate behavior at their college. She soon becomes obsessed with a younger male novelist who comes to speak on campus, Vladimir Vladinski.

TONE IN DIALOGUE AND THOUGHTS

In this exchange, the protagonist is walking with colleagues who casually bring up her husband's trial. She is nonplussed, as she not only downplays his behavior but doesn't think the case will amount to anything. As the conversation continues, notice how the tone changes as her awareness does.

> Content note: Sexual assault /rape

Florence began.

"You know that John's trial begins on the twentieth?"

"His hearing," I corrected.

"Were you planning on attending?"

"No," I said. I was in fact ambivalent, but I didn't want to admit that ambivalence to either of them.

"Good," she said.

David started in. "Look, you know the times we are living in."

"Certainly I do."

"Absurd, you have to be so careful, you get no support from the administration—nothing to back you up—the students rule the roost—you know what I mean."

"What are you getting at? Did I do something wrong? Something offensive?"

Florence shook her head vigorously. "No no no no no no no no no no."

"So then what is it?"

As Florence seemed unable to speak, David nodded at her to show he would take over. If there weren't such a discrepancy of attractiveness between the two, I would think they were together.

"Please, David, just say what you're going to say, this is agonizing," I said.

Without deciding, we all stopped walking.

"A number of students have expressed that, given the circumstances of John's case, they find your presence in the classroom to be objectionable, even triggering. They feel as though you were complicit in the alleged indiscretions. They have asked that you stop teaching classes immediately until the hearing is over. Depending on the verdict, they asked that we then reassess the situation."

A heavy ball sank into the base of my stomach, and my arms and chest tightened in anger. "And what does the department say?"

"We don't think that the students should have the say about who comes and goes here," David said quickly.

"Still," Florence cut in, "we want them to feel heard. Some of the students have suffered sexual assault, and to be in the presence of a rapist's wife—"

"My husband is not a rapist."

"Maybe not according to you—"

"According to anyone."

The protagonist's attitude starts off blasé, the tone light, as though she isn't worried and doesn't even care about what her husband is accused of; she doesn't take the allegations seriously. It's not until her colleagues begin to suggest that there will be consequences for *her*, that her tone changes to alarm, then anger. It should be noted that this protagonist is something of an antihero, someone we aren't necessarily rooting for, but compelled to follow, if that isn't already obvious.

Tone and Content Should Feel Relevant

What you don't want is for readers to say that the tone of your characters' dialogue feels at odds with the tone of your story overall. For example, if your story is heavy or intense, but the character or narrator is *always* joking in dialogue, it might wear on the reader.

Melodrama in Dialogue

Melodrama in dialogue can be subjective, but a good shorthand is dialogue that runs to displays of emotion that seem larger than the moment calls for. Sometimes just calling attention to emotion itself can feel melodramatic. "I've never felt so deeply touched by a thoughtful gesture in my whole life!" a character might emote. Hyperbole—exaggeration—can also create a melodramatic tone (though not always). Common examples include, "The crash was loud enough to wake the dead," or "I'm so hungry, I could eat a horse" but it can be bigger than that, too: "She was the most amazing person he'd ever met."

However, sometimes a character simply *is* melodramatic, and that's the tone you're striving for, so it's not always a bad thing. It can also vary in different cultures and contexts, so again, please remember that my background confers bias around what I think of as melodrama and it may not be true for another.

Tone in Thoughts

As we move into thoughts, let's recall what I discussed in Chapter 5, that there is a fine line between individuated character thoughts and what is called "narrative voice"—understood to be the "authorial voice" that may or may not be directly coming from the characters. Thoughts are specific moments of character knowledge and feelings that are grounded within the character's POV, but there can be gray area and crossover.

Thoughts might also have different stylistic conventions. They can be highlighted in italics to differentiate them. They can be grounded with a tag, such as, "I / he / she / they thought." They frequently occur in first-person POV, even when the overall POV is third person or omniscient.

Thoughts are often used to reveal the main character's more private or secret desires, frustrations, or judgments about other characters or events in the story. Sometimes, thoughts just contain a stream of consciousness that flows through a character's mind. For story purposes, we may want to use thoughts as a tool of omission and tension that can drive tonal contradictions. In other words, the tone of a character's dialogue may conflict with the tone of their thoughts, because characters don't always say what they really think or feel, given different circumstances (as in code-switching).

Here's an example from the psychological thriller called *The Other Black Girl* by Zakiya Dalila Harris. Nella, a young editor at a big New York publisher called Wagner, is used to navigating a largely white group of coworkers, which means treading carefully in what she says to her white boss. She's been asked to edit a novel with a Black woman protagonist written by a white man, and she's struggling because it's full of stereotypes, but her boss loves the book.

In this scene, Nella's thoughts are merged with the narrative voice.

> But everything else about Shartricia's character felt icky—especially her voice, which read as a cross between that of a freed slave and a Tyler Perry character down on her luck. Still, even with all these thoughts swirling in her head, Nella didn't know how exactly to express any of them to the white woman who was sitting in front of her, asking what she thought. The white woman who just happened to be her boss *and*

> Colin's editor.
>
> "I think this book is very ... timely," Nella said, opting for the buzzword that everyone at Wagner liked to hear.

First, we have an example of her thinking honest opinions she doesn't actually say, showing how thoughts can contain a tone that isn't conveyed in dialogue. Second, while the thoughts reveal Nella's voice, the tone is more clearly communicated a little later in the scene, when Hazel, the newly hired and only other Black woman in the company, joins the meeting. Nella thinks she's found an ally, but she's a bit surprised when Hazel seems to play dumb in front of their boss.

> Had the new girl really just admitted that in front of her boss? *That's pretty ballsy of her*, Nella thought, remembering how much she'd downplayed her own inexperience in publishing when she first started. But an explanation for this came to her almost immediately. *Entry-level assistants are liked way more when their bosses think they're blank slates.*

In both passages, we know that the information revealed to us is coming from Nella's POV, but in the italicized sections it sounds a bit more voicey, a bit more like how she might actually speak in a more casual setting. And the tone is sharper. By calling the other woman "ballsy" we get an air of judgment, maybe indignation. It feels more pointed.

Here's another example in which the narrative voice is attributed to the character, which can be read as their thoughts or opinion, but then we drop into a more direct thought that "sounds" even more like the character's voice—and with it comes an even stronger tone. This is from *Mister Impossible*, part of the YA fantasy Dreamer Trilogy by Maggie Stiefvater.

> The memory hadn't been bad when it happened, even though Matthew never liked saying goodbye to her, but it was terrible now because he knew it was the last time he saw her before she died.
>
> *She wasn't your real mother*, Matthew told himself. *She wasn't even Declan's real mother. She was just a dreamt copy.*

Once again, we know that the first paragraph is all Matthew's perspective, but when he starts talking to himself in second person in the next paragraph, "She wasn't your real mother…" it's loaded with more emotion and a tone of self-recrimination and anger at having been betrayed.

Finally, in this next excerpt from Matt Haig's novel *How to Stop Time*, the protagonist has a condition in which he ages so slowly that he looks thirty, but he's over 400 years old and must continually reinvent his life so his secret won't be discovered because there are nefarious people who want to "experiment" on him. In a scene after he's just finished playing the piano, he's reminiscing about the danger of attachments.

> She would smile, and I'd see it in my mind, the smile, and I would dare to feel happy with another human being.
>
> *This is what playing the piano does.*
>
> *This is the danger of it.*
>
> *It makes you human.*
>
> 'Tom?' she says, breaking my reverie. 'Would you like another drink?'

The tone of his thoughts here is bittersweet, full of longing. He's imagining happiness for himself with a woman he cares for, yet knows no relationship is safe because he can't reveal his secret.

I like the way you can play with tonal variances between thoughts and dialogue—showing characters "admit" their real feelings in thoughts while "performing" a different attitude up front, or some variation. While tones can shift throughout a novel, be sure that any tonal shifts are intentional.

In Summary

- **Use dialogue strategically:** Dialogue is a tool that should reveal character emotions, backstory, relationships, and motivations rather than mundane conversation.

- **Dialogue conveys tone:** Use dialogue to layer in tone and subtext, often communicating deeper, unspoken feelings like desire, threat, discomfort, or attraction.

- **Use thoughts for what can't be spoken:** Thoughts represent the private voice of a character, often showing their true feelings or hidden motivations. Characters may code-switch in dialogue or thoughts depending on the context, revealing internal conflict and tension.

- **Avoid melodrama unless intentional:** Overly exaggerated dialogue, hyperbole, emotional drama, and more can undermine authenticity unless it fits the character or story style.

- **Decide how to express thoughts:** Thoughts can appear as narrative voice or internal dialogue, distinguished stylistically through italics or clear attribution like "she thought."

- **Tone must align with overall content:** Inconsistent tone risks distracting readers or detracting from the emotional impact of the story.

VOICE LESSONS

Writing Exercises

Now, you give it a try!

Dialogue Tone Shift

Write a short scene in which two characters are having a conversation. Start with a light, casual tone, but halfway through, shift the tone to something more intense, such as sorrow, jealousy or anger. Focus on how the words and even subtext change to convey the shift in tone but try to keep the dialogue sounding natural. Afterward, reflect on how the tone change impacts the relationship between the characters.

Thoughts vs. Spoken Words

Write a scene in which a character is interacting with someone they don't like or with whom they've had a negative past reaction. Let their thoughts sharply contrast with what they say. For example, the character might be smiling and saying something polite, but in their head, they're thinking a judgment or an insult. Try to capture the difference in tone between their internal monologue and external dialogue.

Character's Public vs. Private Voice

Choose a character—or your own narrator—and write two brief monologues: one in which they speak to another character (dialogue) in a public setting and one in which they express their thoughts privately (internal monologue). Consciously make the tone of their thoughts differ from their speech. For example, maybe they're cordial or professional in the dialogue, but their inner thoughts reveal discomfort, sarcasm, or anger.

"[Poetry] takes us inside situations, helps us imagine life from more than one perspective, honors imagery and metaphor, those great tools of thought, and deepens our confidence in a meaningful world."

—Naomi Shihab Nye

CHAPTER 14

Creating Tone Through Imagery

The Power of Imagery

Isn't it marvelous that writing, little more than squiggles on a page or screen, can evoke entire worlds and fully realized people inside the reader's mind? Voice and tone emerge from these squiggles like incantations of personality and drama, but they do so through a variety of additional techniques as well. One of these techniques is to use imagery, metaphor, and simile to create or highlight the tone you're striving for.

First, here's a quote by Adair Lara, from her book on writing memoir and essay, *Naked, Drunk, and Writing: Shed Your Inhibitions and Craft a Compelling Memoir or Personal Essay:* "If you were a photographer, tone would be the way you light your subject. For dramatic shadows, lit from the side. For a scary effect, from above. For romance, lit with candles. In a movie, tone is often conveyed with music—think of the ominous score accompanying the girl swimming in shark-infested waters in *Jaws*."

What Is Imagery?

Images can be simple descriptions of any sensory experience (that which you can see, hear, touch, taste, feel, or otherwise perceive). They can also be *stylized* to evoke emotional, symbolic, or thematic meaning or to create ambience. They work well in the realm of "show, don't tell."

Imagery can:

- Use description in a symbolic way, through metaphor, simile, or lyrical language.

- Bypass the conscious mind and cut straight to the heart and gut. Think of how some poetry often doesn't immediately make "logical" sense, but it speaks to you at some emotional, even body-centered place instead.

- Communicate emotion in an indirect way, but powerfully. Imagery is often associative—one thing evoking another.

- Tap into deep feelings through visual descriptions. Images are linked to memory, imagination, and, if you believe such a thing exists, perhaps the collective unconscious.

To get more familiar with images, we'll start by looking at one from Karen Russell's coming-of-age novel, *Swamplandia!*

> The Bird Man's eyes were like new lamps for the old performance. He kept smiling and smiling at me, and when his gaze rolled over my skinny legs, the pins of my knees became twin suns.

What tone do you take away from this imagery in which a man's eyes are compared to "new lamps" for "the old performance?" And her skinny legs transform into "twin suns"?

I ask this in my classes without letting anyone know the context of the paragraph, and most people say the tone is of delight or desire in being regarded or admired. He's looking at her in a way that she has never or not for a while been looked at, with fresh intensity. You might even think of it as a light or flirtatious tone.

But now, reread the paragraph with the actual context: The man is a grown adult, and the narrator is a naïve, inexperienced, and isolated teenaged girl. Notice how the tone changes? The tone now feels threatening, ominous. He's regarding her sexually, menacingly, in a way the reader roots *against*. Yet she writes the novel from the girl's POV, so we are inside *her* experience. If an omniscient narrator were telling us the story, it might be laced with the judgment the reader naturally brings to reading it. Instead, we are allowed the character's experience, tonally, which is important to her character arc. It goes to show you that for a reader who has more information than a character, imagery can build in degrees, or layers, of tone.

In this next example, notice the ways Rebecca Lawton, author and former Grand Canyon River guide, uses imagery in her collection of essays about water and the natural world, *The Oasis This Time: Living and Dying with Water in the West*.

> River canyons, especially the Grand Canyon, are places of secrets, too: hidden green grottoes never dreamed of by the sun-dazed visitor who spends the obligatory ten minutes at the South Rim …

Lawton could have written this in a straightforward way, such as: "They're shadowy, green, and off the beaten path." However, her lyrical use of imagery, "hidden green grottoes" (beautiful alliteration) and the image of "sun-dazed visitor" evokes something more than just a little canyon in the river. Its tone beckons readers in, almost magically.

Images as Similes

Images often come in the form of similes—comparing one thing to another (using the words "like" or "as"). The comparison is often where the tone fully comes through.

Here's an example from *Just Last Night* by Mhairi

McFarlane, which is ostensibly a rom-com, but one with a tragedy at its core, seamlessly blending humor with the deeper emotions of grief and regret.

> But the ease with which I can conjure you up, it feels like a curse. A parlor trick, but it's ghoulish, a parody. It's like waltzing with a mannequin.

As the protagonist thinks of her deceased best friend, even the imagery is tonally steeped in that combination of humor and grief. It's when she compares thinking of her friend to "waltzing with a mannequin" that the tone comes through: funny but sad.

This next example from the novel *Age of Vice*, by Deepti Kapoor, an epic crime story that spans decades in India.

> Ajay feels like he's become trapped in a grotesque civil war, and somehow Neda is the cause. He imagines all kinds of vague and terrible things about her. That she has come expressly to ruin Sunny's life, to disrupt the gentle, luxurious harmony that had been put in place. Perhaps she was a spy all along.

The key simile here is "like he's become trapped in a grotesque civil war." The woman, Neda, is the new paramour of Ajay's boss, Sunny, and she creates challenges for him. He's risen from almost nothing and worked his way into a good life through this job, and now this woman threatens it. It's not *just* frustrating, however; Kapoor compares it to conflict akin to civil war, where friends may have to turn on, even kill, one another.

Lastly, we have this simple simile from one of horror master Stephen King's novels, *The Long Walk*: "Either way, or both, he died like a bug under a microscope."

In King's novel, contestants engage in a "grueling walking competition" where the winner is simply the one who survives, and spectators assemble along the way to watch. King's famous for these kinds of stark commentaries on society in his horror. The tone of the simile above feels blunt, as conveyed in the phrase "like a bug under a microscope." Not only does it convey that the young man's death is literally being viewed by millions, but within it is a subtle tone of judgment; people entertained by the tragedy of others are complicit in their deaths.

Images as Metaphors

Metaphors also use imagery, but a metaphor invokes a comparison between things that cannot typically be. Or, as Constance Hale writes in *Sin and Syntax*, "Metaphor surprises us, revealing deeper truths and providing unexpected insights."

Here's an example from the YA novel, *The Fault in Our Stars* by John Green: "My thoughts are stars I cannot fathom into constellations."

On the literal level, thoughts cannot be stars or constellations, but we understand the metaphor to mean a grand bafflement or confusion. In a story that centers on teens with cancer, the tone of emotions at a cosmic scale makes sense.

Here's another example within dialogue from the novel *My Dark Vanessa* by Kate Elizabeth Russell, in which a teen is groomed by her adult English teacher into an "affair" (which I put in quotes because a teen can't consent to such a thing):

> "When we're together," he says, "It feels as though the dark things inside me rise to the surface and brush against the dark things inside you."

The teacher-predator has set his sights on this young woman, whom he knows to be a deeply emotional, troubled girl who reads a lot. He intentionally speaks her language of metaphor, "the dark things inside me / you," as though neither of them can help this taboo allure. He's striving to make her feel seen and heard with the knowledge that he is preying on her, and it also doubles as an indirect confession of his true nature.

Then there's this example from Gina Frangello's memoir, *Blow Your House Down*. After the sudden death of her best friend in her early forties, Frangello is taking stock of what their often tumultuous friendship meant to her in this passage.

> Were we also fun-house mirrors for each other's images and needs?... I wish I could thank her for the ways her skewed vision of me gave me the confidence to take on the world, making me more, even as the loss of her felt like a forensic blue light shining mercilessly on the invisible cracks left behind, not just in my "perfect life" but in me.

The image "fun-house mirrors for each other's images and needs" suggests they had an unreal and "skewed vision" of each other. Then she drops into a simile, comparing her friend's perception of her to a "forensic blue light shining mercilessly on the invisible cracks left behind…" These images all help to create a tone of honesty. In this book, Frangello lays bare her own "failures" and "betrayals." Her tone is never one of self-pity; it's a tone of authenticity and honesty, a tone that suggests anyone who passes judgment isn't admitting their own faults.

Emotional Imagery

Though we explored a little bit in Chapter 3 how imagery can convey emotion, let's look at it again to explain how it can shape the emotional tone of a scene. Images can convey the complexities of emotions too, through their layers.

This next example is from the YA fantasy novel *The Hazel Wood* by Melissa Albert. All you need to know in this scene is that protagonist Alice is watching something happen to her friend, Finch:

> Time slowed. Finch was a spilled cup, just before it hit the ground. A precious something dropped into the dark beneath a subway grate …

The imagery of her friend "as a spilled cup" and "A precious something dropped" give us emotional clues as to the tone or, at least, as to how Alice feels. The tone isn't simply that she's sad or aghast or concerned—it's closer to that stomach-dropping sensation when you are helpless to stop something horrible from happening. The tone is shocked horror.

Here's another image from the same book, also describing Alice's emotions:

> I'd felt for months as though I lived pushed up against glass walls. I couldn't find a way in. Out on the sidewalk, alone, I watched the crowds reveling inside.

The image "I lived pushed up against glass walls" is strikingly revealing. She could have just written that Alice felt lonely or isolated. But the image conveys the tone of isolation more palpably, and allows the emotion to rise inside the reader, rather than being just an intellectual exercise.

Here's one more from the memoir, *Excavation* by Wendy C. Ortiz:

> The stoplight turned green. Cars careened by, people going on dates, stereos happily vibrating the joys of Saturday night. My legs felt like the asphalt the cars were treading on—heavy, fissured, at some breaking point.

The memoir is a (true) story of a teacher who groomed his student, and Ortiz's narrator is constantly grappling with her feelings for the man she thinks she loves. In this scene, she thinks she is breaking up with him, and her emotional experience is conveyed through the image of her legs feeling like asphalt, "heavy, fissured, at some breaking point." We know that doesn't just refer to her legs, but her heart.

Mood Pieces

As Adair Lara's earlier quote suggests, the imagery you use in your scenes can highlight or suggest tone but also create a mood, a sister of tone. Think of imagery as "mood pieces" reinforcing the tone you're creating.

Let's look at two passages that demonstrate these mood pieces from *We Are All the Same in the Dark*, by Julia Heaberlin.

> Trumanell is a shadow on the porch, waiting. The girl's still as a corpse in my arms, the gold scarf glittering around her neck. The sun, at full blare, lights her like she's on fire. You can't tell anything's much wrong with her eyes closed.

The glittering scarf, the sun at full blare, and even the mention of the word "corpse" all create a mood / tone. All we know of Wyatt is that the townspeople think he killed his long-missing sister, Trumanell, years ago. The imagery sets a mood for intensity, danger, and possibly for further harm. We are led to not trust him in this moment.

Here's another excerpt, from the perspective of the young detective, Odette, who has a past with Wyatt:

> The Branson place is rising up in the distance like Moby Dick out of the sea—a big white territorial whale that seems like it scared everything else away. It pretty much did. So I don't have a good feeling. I never do when I head out here. If the house is a killer whale, the past is a maverick shark circling its body, waiting for me.

Here, we're steeped in ocean imagery: Moby Dick, a territorial whale, a maverick shark. The imagery suggests adversity already, a mood of conflict ensuing, past and present, and possibly future. It's a tense mood, a fearful tone, and it sets the reader on edge.

Tone Conveyed Through Setting

In the same vein as "mood pieces," setting is another way you can load imagery to convey tone in a given scene. Think about how a change in lighting or weather, or a focus on colors or patterns can shift the feeling of a scene, and setting-as-mood will start to become obvious.

In this passage from Mindy Mejia's literary crime novel, *Leave No Trace*, notice the way the setting matches the emotions of protagonist Maya Stark. Maya has been abandoned by her mother, who suffered depression and suicidal ideation before she disappeared. The following passage is a memory of a good time she spent with her mother.

> During Dad's busy season in the summer, Mom took me up to her family cabin near the Boundary Waters, and that's where she seemed the strongest. We paddled through lake after lake, silent amid the towering pines that surrounded us like a cathedral, our feet baptized on the shores of every portage. When we returned to Duluth in the fall, everything seemed dirtier, harder.

Notice that when the narrator is with her mother in nature, the descriptions are full of an expansive beauty and sense of openness through descriptions that compare the "towering pines" to a cathedral, and their feet aren't just wet, they're "baptized on the shores of every portage." The mood is one of peace and reverence, and the tone, if not quite joyful, is perhaps contented.

Contrast that with the tone of the final line about when they returned home to Duluth, which is also when Mom slips into her depression again, and the narrator describes it as "dirtier, harder."

Note that tone doesn't have to be created through complex or lengthy passages—sometimes it's as simple as a single paragraph or sentence.

Let's look at one more example that allows the individual tone of each character to come through via the imagery of the setting.

This example comes from Tana French's novel *The Secret Place*, set in Dublin, Ireland.

Detective Stephen Moran is a working-class guy stuck in Cold Cases but he secretly covets the more prestigious Murder department. When he discovers a clue that reopens a cold case, he gets his chance, and takes it to Detective Antoinette Conway, finally breaking into the Murder Squad.

In this scene, they first lay eyes on the girls' private school where they have come to conduct a series of key interviews. The first version is from Moran's POV.

CREATING TONE THROUGH IMAGERY

> I started to ask something, but Conway spun the car into a turn—so sudden, no blinker, I almost missed the moment we crossed over: high black-iron gates, stone guardhouse, iron arch with "St. Kilda College" picked out in gold. Inside the gates she braked. Let me take a good look.
>
> Someone's ancestral home, once, someone's mansion with grooms holding dancing carriage horses, with tiny-waisted ladies drifting arm in arm across the grass. Two hundred years old, more? A long building, soft gray stone, three tall windows up and more than a dozen across. A portico held up by slim curl-topped columns; a rooftop balustrade, pillars curved delicate as vases. Perfect, it was; perfect, everything balanced, every inch. Sun melting over it, slow as butter on toast.

Moran's tone is full of awe and respect for this institution. He's so homed in on the details, it's like he's become a scholar of architecture—noting its black iron, its stone guardhouse, its gold letters. And he waxes positively novelistic in his imaginations of who might have once lived there, imagining "tiny-waisted ladies" and dancing carriage horses" and all of it "perfect, everything balanced, every inch." I always note how he thinks "I almost missed the moment we crossed over" as though it would have been a tragedy if he hadn't noticed all these details. Moran holds this school, and the wealth and privilege it stands for, in great esteem; it represents the status that he would like to obtain.

Now, contrast that with Conway's POV, in which a totally different tone comes through (one that is highlighted in its drama, because we've already seen Moran's absurdly gushing review of the school).

She tells Moran: "This is the only time I'm sorry I'm a cop. When I see a shitpile like this and I can't petrol-bomb it to fuck."

Conway's tone is not just unimpressed, but angry and negative. The reader will eventually learn that Conway has a personal relationship with this school, and it wasn't a happy place for her.

Thus, setting is used here to reflect a tone or attitude that the characters hold.

Thematic Imagery and Tone

The last way we'll talk about using imagery to convey tone is through thematic imagery. Because of images' ability to convey information indirectly, poetically, and from unique angles, they are wonderful at evoking theme. Themes, of course, are the underlying or overarching messages of your story: Forgiveness, redemption, unconditional love, overcoming oppression—imagine what sorts of images might reflect them and weave them in.

Say your theme is finding your voice, as in courage or strength. What might be some images that convey this? Remember, an image is either a metaphor, a simile, a symbol, or a descriptive passage.

- Song or speech

- Things that stand tall or proud, like trees or pillars, or even spines

Thematic imagery works best when it is subtle, planted in the backdrop or the subtext of a scene.

Here's some thematic imagery from Addie Tsai's novel *Unwieldy Creatures*, described as a "gender-swapped, queer, biracial retelling of *Frankenstein*."

> Each piece of the body born into my possession gradually taken, the right to do with it what I chose gone without warning, like a thief in the black cape of night. What is a life, after all, without a body to call your own.

And:

> Like you, I'm also a Venn diagram of blood and body. I was born in West Texas by a white man and a brown woman from Jakarta.

In Tsai's Frankenstein retelling, the body / bodies are the center of the story, both literally and metaphorically, as Dr. Frank, a non-binary person, strives to create a baby without the aid of a man. The book is rich with explorations of the limits of gender binaries and the impositions of state laws upon bodies and the imagery never shies away from its serious but also idealistic tone.

Lastly, let's look at the thematic imagery from R.O. Kwon's *The Incendiaries* again, in which protagonist Will's girlfriend, Phoebe, has become involved with a religious cult.

In this passage, after the characters first sleep together, we see Phoebe through Will's eyes:

> In the morning, I watched as she slept, netted in white sheets. Nostrils flared with each long inhale. Pearl studs glinted at slim earlobes. Minute, fish-scale veins patterned Phoebe's eyelids in faint blue. … In the old-gold light of morning, I had the idea she might have been a wild sea-creature who'd washed onshore, luck's gift, legs tucked like a mermaid's tail. I learned to swim before I could walk, she said.

The imagery all points to Phoebe being fishlike, slippery, something wild and impossible to pin down, like a mermaid. It's a melancholy tone, since Will spends much of the book chasing Phoebe, trying to grasp her back from the clutches of the cult—the images are thematic perfection.

If you feel you're not quite nailing tone during the first draft, rest assured that you'll have time to consider it in revision and can refine and tweak it as much as necessary. Sometimes, having a completed draft can make it easier to see and hear the tone you're striving to create.

In Summary

- **Imagery contributes to tone:** Visual and sensory imagery evokes emotional, symbolic, and thematic meaning, helping to establish tone.

- **Similes and metaphors shape tone:** Comparisons through similes or metaphors also convey tone by comparing disparate things and eliciting feelings more subtly.

- **Tone shifts:** Tone can shift depending on context and point of view, as illustrated through imagery (the same imagery feeling flirtatious or menacing, depending on the narrator's perspective).

- **Mood pieces:** Imagistic mood pieces can shape or complement the tone, influencing the reader's emotional experience of the scene (setting descriptions influencing the emotional tone of a scene or the characters' emotions).

- **Thematic imagery:** Imagery can reflect deeper themes in the story (identity, body autonomy) in subtle ways, enriching the underlying message without being overt.

- **Contextual impact:** The emotional tone and mood are often influenced by the specific context in which the imagery appears, such as character backstories or the nature of the setting.

VOICE LESSONS

Writing Exercises

Now, you give it a try!

Symbolic Imagery

Choose an object that means something to your character or has thematic resonance within your story, such as a flower, a clock, or a broken mirror, and write a short paragraph describing it from the POV of a character or narrator in your work. Use metaphor or simile to imbue the object with deeper symbolic meaning. Aim to create an emotional tone without explicitly stating it. For example, if you're using a broken clock, you might describe it as "the hands frozen at midnight, like a heart that's forgotten how to beat."

Tone Shifts

Write two short scenes using the same imagery, but from different perspectives. In one version, describe the imagery from a hopeful or romantic point of view; in the other, write the same imagery from a fearful or ominous perspective. For example, describe a sunset or a dark alley, first as a place of comfort and beauty, and then as a site of danger or dread. Pay attention to how the tone changes with the emotional context of the character.

Mood Pieces and Setting

Write a short scene in which the setting creates a mood, such as a rainy street, a forest, a crowded subway. Use descriptive language that reflects both the physical environment and the emotions of the character. For example, you could describe the setting as "the steady drizzle softened the world, turning everything into a blurred watercolor painting," and then show how the character's feelings shift due to the weather (perhaps feeling lost or comforted).

"Good stories are good stories, no matter how they're categorized."

—Octavia E. Butler

CHAPTER 15

Tone in Genre

Tone in Fiction Genres

If the hard genres stress you out, first consider that they are as much about marketing categories as they are legitimate expectations that readers hold. If a reader goes in expecting "romantasy," you must deliver, but a ripping good tale can also defy genre.

It's also not helpful to relate to tone in an anxious way, or to be fearful that the demands of your genre will only allow for a limited tone you can't stray from. While it's true that some genres are very specific in their tastes, focus more on telling a story in the way that feels right to you. Think of genre as a gentle guideline to nudge you in the right direction.

In this chapter, we'll discuss how much tone can vary within a genre (and this includes memoir).

Epic Fantasy

We'll start by looking at the tone differences in two epic fantasy novels, *Empire of the Vampire* by Jay Kristoff and *Strange the Dreamer* by Laini Taylor. Both are set in alternate worlds / realities and timelines from our own with their own unique worldbuilding.

Empire of the Vampire starts like this:

> It was the twenty-seventh year of daysdeath in the realm of the Forever King, and his murderer was waiting to die.
>
> The killer stood watch at a thin window, impatient for his end to arrive. Tattooed hands were clasped at his back, stained with dried blood and ashes pale as starlight. His room stood high in the reaches of a lonely tower, kissed by sleepless mountain winds. The door was ironclad, heavy, locked like a secret. From his vantage, the killer watched the sun sink toward an unearned rest and wondered how hell might taste.

The tone of *Empire of the Vampire* is heavy, somber, and weighted with the character's mortality as he waits to die. The very name of the year "daysdeath" brings a sense of foreboding, as does his self-punitive judgments of "an unearned rest" and wondering how "hell might taste." You don't expect a lighthearted romp out of this read.

Now, let's contrast it with *Strange the Dreamer*:

> Names may be lost or forgotten. No one knew that

better than Lazlo Strange. He'd had another name first, but it had died like a song with no one left to sing it. Maybe it had been an old family name, burnished by generations of use. Maybe it had been given to him by someone who loved him. He liked to think so, but he had no idea. All he had were *Lazlo* and *Strange*—*Strange* because that was the surname given to all foundlings in the Kingdom of Zosma, and *Lazlo* after a monk's tongueless uncle.

In Taylor's book, though the character has every right to feel self-pitying or despairing based on the description of his past as a "foundling" whose original name had "no one left to sing it", it doesn't. The tone is dreamy, almost mythical.

Two epic fantasy novels with male protagonists, two very different tones. Notice too how many of the elements we've discussed that shape voice come through: character opinions, manner of expression, history, personality, and more.

Mysteries and Thrillers

Who doesn't love a good mystery or thriller? You might expect most of them to have gritty, serious, or intense tones. While plenty of them do, they can also vary in tone.

Check out the way Megan Abbott's psychological thriller *You Will Know Me* begins:

> **Go Devon! Knox Rox! Next Stop: Elite Qualifiers!**
>
> **Belstars 4-Ever! Regional Champs!**
>
> The viny banners rippled from the air vent, the restaurant roiling with parents, the bobbing of gymnast heads, music gushing from the weighty speakers keeled on the window ledges.
>
> Slung around Devon's neck were three medals, two silver and one gold, her first regional-champion title on the vault.
>
> "I'm so proud of you, sweetie," Katie whispered in her daughter's ear. "You can do anything."

If you didn't know anything about this book, the tone could read like the opening to a middle-grade novel, a literary novel, or a coming-of-age story. There's very little in the chipper "go-go" tone that sets it apart as a psychological thriller until the next paragraph when the line, "Later, Katie would come to think of that night as the key to everything that came after, the secret code," gives us a hint of more to come.

Then there's this example from Sarah Pinborough's psychological thriller *Behind Her Eyes*:

> Pinch myself and say I AM AWAKE once an hour.
>
> Look at my hands. Count my fingers.
>
> Look at clock (or watch), look away, look back.
>
> Stay calm and focused.

Think of a door.

The tone contrast with *You Will Know Me* is dramatic—these short, clipped sentences create a feeling of urgency, as though the narrator doesn't trust herself to follow simple instructions. The repetition of actions "look at clock, look away, look back" and the final, almost cryptic command, "Think of a door," add an eerie or dreamlike quality that is decidedly not there in the Abbott example. The fact that this is the entire chapter, with nothing else to ground the reader, adds a creepy vibe.

Here's a third one from Tess Gerritsen's thriller *The Spy Coast* with yet another tone:

> She used to be the golden girl. *How things have changed,* she thought, staring in the mirror. Her hair, once artfully streaked with sun-kissed highlights, was now what could only be described as dead-mouse brown. It was the most unobtrusive shade of hair color she could find on the shelves at the Monoprix, where she'd gone shopping after a neighbor mentioned that a man had been asking about her. That was the first clue that something might be amiss, that someone was asking about her, although there could have been a completely innocent explanation. He might have been an admirer, or a man trying to make a delivery, but she did not want to be caught unprepared, so she'd headed across town to a Monoprix in the third arrondissement, a neighborhood where no one knew her, and she'd bought hair color and eyeglasses. These were items she should always have kept on hand, but over

the years she'd grown complacent. Careless.

The tone starts out self-deprecating. It could be a setup for any kind of contemporary story—a rom-com, a comedy, or a lighthearted contemporary story as she assesses herself and finds herself coming up short. However, as the paragraph progresses, a sense of unease creeps in with the line "someone was asking about her," introducing an element of suspense. That she would dye her hair over something so simple signals a tone change coming, which arrives in the lines "but over the years she'd grown complacent. Careless." The tone is creeping steadily toward a more serious one.

Tone in Memoir and Essay

Let's jump over into memoir for a moment, which, as genre goes, is a bit like lumping every different kind of fruit under the sun into the category of "nutrients." Even though memoir tends to be sold as one category, there are as many different types of memoirs as there are people writing them.

One gritty and gripping memoir is *Madness: A Bipolar Life* by Marya Hornbacher, chronicling her reckoning with bipolar disease and alcohol misuse. It opens with a prologue that puts us right in the middle of one of her worst moments.

TONE IN GENRE

> Content note: Self-harm and blood

> I am numb. I am in the bathroom of my apartment in Minneapolis, twenty years old, drunk, and out of my mind. I am cutting patterns in my arm, a leaf and a snake. There is one dangling light, a bare bulb with a filthy string that twitches in the breeze coming through the open window. I look out on an alley and the brick buildings next door, all covered with soot. Across the way a woman sits on her sagging flowered couch in her slip and slippers, watching TV, laughing along with the laugh track, and I stop to sop up the blood with a rag. The blood is making a mess on the floor (note to self: mop floor) while a raccoon clangs the lid of a dumpster down below. Time hiccups; it is either later or sooner, I can't tell which. I study my handiwork. Blood runs down my arm, wrapping around my wrists and dripping off my fingers onto the dirty white tile floor.

I would describe the tone of her book as unflinching and direct. She doesn't shy away from telling it like it is, without flourish or poetry. It's direct and clear, a tone that tells us we will likely get the unvarnished truth.

Now, in contrast, here are some excerpts from one of the essays that compose Anne Liu Kellor's gorgeous memoir-in-essays *Heart Radical: A Search for Language, Love, and Belonging*, titled "Mirror Face."

> Every woman who lives in a house has a mirror face. A way she examines her reflection, tilts her head, casts her eyes, gauges her own appearance. After putting

> on makeup or combing her hair, she makes a final assessment of how she appears—or rather, what she thinks she looks like to others—before she walks out the door into public.
>
> My mirror face took hold in middle school, a time when I became obsessed by how I was seen. Every morning I rushed to the bathroom mirror to see whether my eyes would match or not. The left lid always had a crease in the middle, like a Westerner's eye, but the right eyelid would sometimes grow puffy and fail to fold on days when I hadn't gotten enough rest. At the time, I did not think of my creaseless eye as looking more "Chinese" but I did know it made me look sleepier or uglier.

The tone begins in a more detached manner as Kellor ruminates on traits that sound almost universal, describing women engaging with their own image in a world that judges them on their beauty. The tone is analytical (though the sentence-level writing, with its rhythmic cadence, feels poetic). As she shifts toward more personal experiences as a Chinese American girl in a Western school, the tone grows melancholy. We can read into the phrases "obsessed by how I was seen" and "sleepier or uglier" that experiences as a woman of color in a white-dominant society have caused her pain.

Lastly in the memoir category, let's look at the tone of Terese Marie Mailhot's *Heart Berries*, about her coming of age as a Native American woman on the Seabird Island Indian reservation.

> My story was maltreated. The words were too wrong and ugly to speak. I tried to tell someone my story, but he thought it was a hustle. He marked it as solicitation. The man took me shopping with his pity. I was silenced by charity—like so many Indians. I kept my hand out. My story became the hustle.
>
> Women asked me what my endgame was. I hadn't thought about it. I considered marrying one of the men and sitting with my winnings, but I was too smart to sit. I took their money and went to school. I was hungry and took more. When I gained the faculty to speak my story, I realized I had given men too much.

Mailhot's tone is almost mythic, expanding her own experience into something bigger and even separate from her, an entity all its own. "My story was maltreated" as if it were a child, or an animal. Mailhot's tone slingshots between fury and ferocity throughout the book as she explores the ways she both had no control over things in her own life and tried to take control of what she could.

Hopefully this chapter has revealed that even books in the same genre can have a wide variety of tones. While the firmer the genre demands are, the greater publishers' expectations of voice and tone, there's fortunately so much gray area that writers have a lot more room to play.

In Summary

- **Genre is a guideline:** While genres do influence tone, if you are a genre-straddler, remember to view them more as marketing categories and guidelines rather than rigid rules.

- **Tone varies within genres:** Tone can vary significantly within the same genre, so long as you're doing it intentionally.

- **Memoir tone variety:** Memoirs can also adopt a wide array of tones, from unflinchingly direct and gritty) to poetic and reflective.

- **Genre expectations for tone:** While publishers may have specific expectations about tone within genres, there is significant gray area that allows writers to creatively experiment with tone and voice, giving them room to push boundaries while still staying within genre conventions.

VOICE LESSONS

Writing Exercises

Now, you give it a try!

Tone Shifting

PROMPT:

Choose a scene from your current work in progress or write a new scene involving a character in a difficult situation (such as waiting for a life-changing event, a tense conversation, or a moment of introspection).

- First, write the scene with a somber, heavy tone, focusing on the character's emotional weight and inner turmoil.

- Then, rewrite the same scene with a lighthearted or whimsical tone, focusing on humor or irony while keeping the core elements of the situation.

Genre Tone Comparison

PROMPT:

Write the first paragraph of a story in three different genres (epic fantasy, mystery, memoir). For each genre, adjust the tone to fit the conventions of the genre, even if it means shifting the content of the scene.

- For epic fantasy, write a grand and dramatic introduction (such as a character facing an impending battle or supernatural event).

- For mystery, create a tense or eerie moment, perhaps with an ominous hint of danger or a puzzle to be solved.

Memoir Tone Exploration

PROMPT:

Write a short memoir-like reflection about a personal experience, but vary the tone based on the following instructions:

- **Option 1:** Write the memory with a detached, analytical tone, focusing on factual details and objective observations.

- **Option 2:** Rewrite the memory, reflecting on the emotional impact the event had on you at the time.

- **Option 3:** Finally, rewrite the same memory with an angry or frustrated tone, focusing on the injustice or emotional turmoil the event may have stirred up.

PART FOUR

Final Voice Notes

"When we are objective we are subjective too. When we are neutral we are involved. When we say 'I think' we don't leave our emotions outside the door. To tell someone not to be emotional is to tell them to be dead."

—Jeanette Winterson, *Why Be Happy When You Could Be Normal?*

CHAPTER 16

Voice in Nonfiction. Balancing Objectivity and Personality

Voice in Nonfiction

Memoir and essay fall into the wide, general category of nonfiction, which is shorthand for "based in fact." However, there are as many kinds of nonfiction as there are topics of interest on Earth, so there's no way to cover all types in this one chapter. Most people have had the experience of reading something so dry and voiceless that you're glazing over a paragraph, so you understand the importance of a memorable voice in something that could otherwise bore.

Not to mention, in an era when many more people are turning to nonexperts with a camera and a selfie stick on social media for their information, it's more important than ever to make your nonfiction compelling.

Balance the Factual with the Personal

To begin this section, I want to tell you a story about how I was a mostly failed math student in school all my life, but scored one brilliant, solo "A" in a required math class in college for those who had done poorly on the math entrance exam. The class was called Math for Liberal Arts Students. Could any class have been more tailor-made for me!?

I traipsed in with low expectations, prepared to feel dumb again in the face of yet more formulas my brain wouldn't grasp, but was pleasantly surprised. Instead of complex formulas I was supposed to memorize quickly, our professor told stories about the people behind the math—their lives, their breakthroughs, their journeys, and even their philosophies as they discovered and created their mathematical formulas.

The human element woke the subject for me. While the whole idea behind nonfiction might seem to be facts first, sometimes adding the personal angle brings a reader in more deeply. Not only did I earn that A, but I also understood a couple of those formulas for the first time ever.

To illustrate the way the personal can enhance the factual, let's begin by looking at an incredible nonfiction example in Chanda Prescod-Weinstein's book about physics, politics, and being a Black woman in America, *The Disordered Cosmos: A Journey into Dark Matter, Spacetime, & Dreams Deferred*.

VOICE IN NONFICTION. BALANCING OBJECTIVITY AND PERSONALITY

Prescod-Weinstein is one of around 100 Black American women to earn a PhD from a department of physics. So, this is a book teaching readers about physics, but it is also a cosmology of her own experiences as a Black woman and a science nerd, in the US.

> The story goes like this. Me: Black child on a school bus that is slowly crawling along the 10 Freeway East, windows down, exhaust filling her nose and lungs, causing headaches that stop only years later when her dreams of particle physics carry her far away from the Los Angeles smog. I am reading and then taking breaks from reading to tell whoever is left on the bus—just a handful of children because between my school's grades six through twelve, only about four of us live this far away—about these things called quarks. I don't know what a quark is or where the name comes from. I don't particularly care about the name either. But I know that the world is made out of quarks. I know that my brain is a quark and electron collection.

Because she brings us into her own personal story, readers immediately know this will not be a dry recounting of physics details. The voice is personal, the tone intimate and inviting, beckoning readers into her experience with the context that we also might learn a few things (which we do).

In another paragraph, she writes about dark matter:

> Today dark matter is one of the two great mysteries in cosmological physics. Occasionally scientists claim that dark matter sounds scary and foreboding to the

> general public. Actually, I've only ever heard white scientists make this claim, and whenever it happens I wonder if that's really telling us more about the way they relate to the idea of "dark." In my view, dark matter is extremely benign.

The personal experience added around the seams of the factual warms the subject matter, making it accessible. Some readers might struggle to connect with this material if it was all fact and no personal information.

Another example of blending the personal with the factual comes from Rebecca Lawton's collection of essays, *Reading Water: Lessons From the River*, about her years as one of the first women river guides.

Lawton beautifully (and I do mean beautifully) weaves her personal stories with scientific facts gleaned from her training as a fluvial geologist, creating a book that is both deeply concerned with revering and protecting the natural world, and one that plumbs the human condition.

> I've always thought that life's like the river, but anybody can see that. There are backwaters and shallows, bridges and dams. There are smooth parts and rough parts. There's the tongue, the smooth "V" pointing to entry for boats, usually followed by rough, bucked-up water in rapids. The tongue, for all its glassy tranquility, accelerating toward chaos. With all its metaphors of probing, licking, and truth-telling. Once you're on the tongue, you're committed. There are no brakes—you have to ride it out.

In Blossom that day, riding it out meant feeling a wooden boat crash down on my back in the middle of a river in flood. Being sucked straight down by the water tugging on my boots—staying down so long and tumbling around so much I doubted I'd see daylight again.

Bringing in a personal element to nonfiction can keep it from being dull or dry. Stylistic elements, too, like Lawton's use of imagery, alliteration, and intentional sentence variety, heightens the reading experience.

Humor and Playfulness

If you're writing a nonfiction book about a serious topic, that doesn't mean you have to take a serious tone all the time, either. Tone can invite in or shut a reader out of an experience. As a cisgender woman going through perimenopause, when I began to search for resources to explain and support my very long list of symptoms that included sudden rage bursts, brain fog, hot flashes and night sweats, itchy ears, bloating, weight gain, and loss of energy and giving a shit, I sure as hell did not want a dry textbook about what was going on with me.

I encountered the delightfully named *What Fresh Hell Is This? Perimenopause, Menopause, Other Indignities, and You* by Heather Corinna, and I knew I had found the book for me because of its voice.

Part One begins with a little epigraph that had me chuckling already: "And in the beginning was the word and the word was 'Dammit.'" Chapter One opens:

> Did you see the title and flame-filled cover of this book, and did your weary, sweaty, confused, and exasperated soul scream, **That one! That is the book for me!!**?
>
> If so, I'd first like to extend my deepest sympathies, an ice pack, and some of these very helpful edibles. If it's three in the morning as you're reading this, as it may well be, you likely want those more than a book. But since I can't really give you the other stuff, I can at least offer you this book until the sun comes up, and you can go get your own coping necessities, whatever they may be.

While some people might want a medical textbook when researching their perimenopause symptoms, I was well past the point of seriousness and ready to laugh at myself, so I didn't cry (as much). And that's not an uncommon scenario, I've since learned, in talking to numerous peri- and menopausal people. Corinna hits that nerve in her book and takes the tone of a good friend, there to share your misery with you and make you laugh while doing so. It's a friendly voice, a relatable voice, and one that someone in the miserable throes of hormone changes might find more welcoming than a clinical voice.

It doesn't stop her from imparting more helpful information, either. Sometimes she stays in the fun voice, like so:

> How do you know if you're in perimenopause?
>
> You can't reliably test for perimenopause most of the time.

> Figuring this out is more like following the rules of the Final Destination franchise. It's about looking for the signs, whether the person looking is you, a healthcare provider, or both. And if you hear John Denver playing, run.

Other times, she gets more serious:

> Because hormones and their levels are all over the place in perimenopause, but levels are also very fluid premenopause, there's usually just no point in running a test because those levels can be so different from day to day either way.

As is probably evidenced by how often I have quoted her, I adore Constance Hale's grammar book *Sin and Syntax* for the way it avoids being yet another dusty tome on grammar.

If there's anything drier than grammar instruction, I'm not sure what it is, yet Hale's voice from the get go is never dull.

> Driven by some combustible mix of passion (for the power and poetry of words) and desperation (so many snags in your sentences!) you've picked up a book called *Sin and Syntax*. What, you're wondering, does syntax—that collection of prissy grammar rules dictating how to put words together—have to do with sin—the reckless urge to flout the rules and abandon propriety altogether?

She tackles the boring nature of grammar head on and challenges you to consider it more interesting than you previously thought. Just like my experience of math throughout school, sometimes a subject isn't so much inherently boring as it's hampered by the way it's taught.

Objectivity and Bias

As both a journalist and a novelist, I'm intimately familiar with the unique variations in writing fact over fiction, how difficult it is to maintain true objectivity, and the subtle ways bias can creep into writing even when you try to keep it out.

Objectivity is harder than it seems, because most of the time we don't even see our own biases; we're too deeply steeped in them. Some would say it's almost impossible to completely remove bias, but being aware of your biases is most important in anything that seeks to educate, inform, or present a balanced agenda. It's not always a bad thing. We often read for someone's bias.

Here's an example from the book by Atul Gawande, a practicing surgeon, who examines the way the current medical system (grounded within US culture) treats death, and thus life.

> This is a book about the modern experience of mortality—about what it's like to be creatures who age and die, how medicine has changed the experience and how it hasn't, where our ideas about how to deal with our finitude have got the reality wrong. As I pass a decade in surgical practice and become middle-aged myself, I find that neither I nor my patients find our current

state tolerable. But I have also found it unclear what the answers should be, or even whether any adequate ones are possible. I have the writer's and scientist's faith, however, that by pulling back the veil and peering in close, a person can make sense of what is most confusing or strange or disturbing.

The reader goes into the reading knowing that Dr. Gawande has direct experience of the medical system, so the book cannot possibly be unbiased, and he doesn't try to suggest otherwise. However, his experience also gives him expertise and a vantage point that someone objective could not have in writing about this same topic.

We also need to be careful about striving for "false balance," which can give voice to incorrect or harmful points of view just in service of being unbiased. According to a 2016 article[8] in *The Guardian*, journalist David Robert Grimes writes, "This situation, known as false balance, arises when journalists present opposing view-points as being more equal than the evidence allows. But when the evidence for a position is virtually incontrovertible, it is profoundly mistaken to treat a conflicting view as equal and opposite by default. With respect to man-made climate change, the BBC is far from the only outlet skewing their coverage in the name of balance, and global coverage on climate science remains exceptionally off-kilter with the scientific consensus."

The same article points out that how not long after the debate about whether the measles-mumps-rubella (MMR) vaccine "caused" autism (a fact that has been uncategorically debunked), journalists and writers with no scientific background were suddenly writing articles on the topic such that, "Suddenly we were getting comment and advice on complex matters of immunology and epidemiology from people who would more usually have been telling us about a funny thing that happened with the au pair on the way to a dinner party."

Opening the Door to Difficult Conversations

Another way to consider the voice you take in nonfiction is if you're writing about something difficult that might challenge the reader in one way or another. A book that had a big impact on me is *My Grandmother's Hands: Radicalized Trauma and the Pathway to Mending Our Hearts and Bodies* by Resmaa Menakem. The book is described as "the first self-help book to examine white body supremacy in America from the perspective of trauma and body-centered psychology." I read it not long after the George Floyd protests, when many Black people I knew were feeling that no matter how much suffering they experienced, white people simply didn't "get it."

Menakem is a former counselor with extensive trauma training, as well as the former behavioral health director for African American Family Services in Minneapolis.

VOICE IN NONFICTION. BALANCING OBJECTIVITY AND PERSONALITY

Though he brings a lot of incredible somatic and psychological expertise to the book that aims to help both white and Black people get on the path to healing racial trauma and division, he also invokes personal stories, like the one that gave this book its name.

He tells of how he used to watch television with his grandmother, who would ask him to rub her hands:

> She wasn't a large woman, but her hands were surprisingly stout with broad fingers and thick pads below each thumb. One day I asked her, "Grandma, why are your hands like that? They ain't the same as mine."

And:

> My grandmother turned from the television and looked at me. "Boy," she said slowly. "That's from picking cotton. They been that way since long before I was your age. I started working in the fields sharecroppin' when I was four."

In this exchange, Menakem drives home several important points: that the effects of slavery and racism linger not just in attitudes, but in the bodies of its survivors and their descendants. He posits that everyone can become aware and change. These are tough topics for some people (of any race) to hear. The storytelling helps the reader connect, so that when he delves into the more clinical information, we're still reading.

> Our bodies have a form of knowledge that is different from our cognitive brains. This knowledge is typically

experienced as a felt sense of constriction or expansion, pain or ease, energy or numbness. Often this knowledge is stored in our bodies as wordless stories about what is safe and what is dangerous.

Striking the right balance between objective and subjective experience can be challenging. It might help to imagine how you want your audience to view you when they're reading your work. Similarly, how do you want them to feel when they read your work? Do you want them to feel lectured to, invited into a conversation, like a child in school, or like a trusted friend? These kinds of considerations will shape the tone of your nonfiction.

Instructional Nonfiction

This book you're reading right now falls into this category of instructional nonfiction in the category of writing craft. I always strive to create a voice that is both clear and helpful but also let a little bit of my personality ooze through the cracks, so you can sense there's a person behind the words and not AI, for example.

Instructional how-to can feel dry, so it's important to infuse as much energy into it as possible, perhaps to even imagine that you're in the room teaching or chatting rather than lecturing at a distance.

A writer who does a great job of this is Jessica Brody in the writing craft book, *Save the Cat! Writes a Novel: The*

VOICE IN NONFICTION. BALANCING OBJECTIVITY AND PERSONALITY

Last Book on Novel Writing You'll Ever Need, based on the work of Blake Snyder.

I have the good fortune of calling Jessica a friend, so it's fun to read the book and catch those bits of her personality I've come to know. Jessica is optimistic, helpful, organized, and really good at what she does. For eager novelists hoping to write the best book possible and improve their chances of publication, they deserve a book that can clearly and helpfully do that.

In Chapter One, "Why Do We Care? Creating the Story-Worthy Hero", Jessica does a great job of making this seem feasible:

> The relationship between character and plot is an essential one. It's why we start the Save the Cat! methodology here, with the main character, who from here on out I will be referring to as the **hero** of your story. Because doesn't that just sound better? A hero is proactive and important and worthy of having an entire novel revolve around them. In the world of Save the Cat!, we write about memorable characters who do memorable stuff. But most of all, we create heroes (male and female!) who are destined to be the center of a plot.
>
> So who is destined to be the center of your plot? Let's roll up our sleeves and find out!

I love how those very qualities I know in Jessica come through in her voice in the book. She is cheerleading the writer on, speaking in a relatable way that doesn't position her in a hierarchy above the reader, even though she has published more than fifteen books and runs a well-regarded writing academy, the Writing Mastery Academy. She's encouraging and inviting, and it makes the reader want to dig right in.

Weaving in Mythology and Other Stories

Some nonfiction authors utilize other myths or stories to enhance, illustrate, or otherwise tell a new story.

Robin Wall Kimmerer is a botanist, author of the book *Braiding Sweetgrass: Indigenous Wisdom, Scientific Knowledge, and the Teachings of Plants*, and a member of the Citizen Potawatomi Nation. She weaves indigenous mythology with science and personal experiences to discuss the many kinds of lenses through which ecology and nature can be viewed. In the chapter titled "Skywoman Falling", she gives us a story that comes from oral tradition of her tribe:

> She fell like a maple seed, pirouetting on an autumn breeze. A column of light streamed from a hole in the Skyworld, marking her path where only darkness had been before. It took her a long time to fall. In fear, or maybe hope, she clutched a bundle tightly in her hand.

Later in the chapter, she connects that story to indigenous peoples' understanding of nature before modern scientists brought their own interpretations.

> Our stories say that of all the plants, wiingaashk, or sweetgrass, was the very first to grow on the earth,

its fragrance a sweet memory of Skywoman's hand. Accordingly, it is honored as one of the four sacred plants of my people. Breathe in its scent and you start to remember things you didn't know you'd forgotten.

Another example of utilizing mythology to illustrate larger points about women and their empowerment, comes from the well-known "self-help" book *Women Who Run With the Wolves: Myths and Stories of the Wild Woman Archetype*, by Clarissa Pinkola Estés, Ph.D.

In almost every chapter, she resurrects a variety of cross-cultural fairy tales and myths to illustrate knowledge she holds as a Jungian psychoanalyst to help women connect to deep, intuitive, and sometimes "lost" parts of themselves.

In Chapter 3, "Nosing Out the Facts: The Retrieval of Intuition as Initiation", Estés draws upon the Russian tale "Vasalisa."

> Intuition is the treasure of a woman's psyche. It is like a divining instrument and like a crystal through which one can see with uncanny interior vision. It is like a wise old woman who is with you always, who tells you exactly what the matter is, tells you exactly whether you need to go left or right. It is a form of The One Who Knows, old La Que Sabe, the Wild Woman.

Then she drops into a version of "Vasalisa."

> Once there was, and once there was not, a young mother who lay on her deathbed, her face pale as the

white wax roses in the sacristy of the church nearby. Her young daughter and her husband sat at the end of her old wooden bed and prayed that God would guide her safely into the next world.

The dying mother called to Vasalisa, and the little child in red boots and white apron knelt at her mother's side.

In both Kimmerer's and Estés's books, the myths and stories layer in additional meaning or provide a context from which to widen an understanding.

If you're writing nonfiction, think of the ways you can bring voice, personality, and personal storytelling to the text so that you capture your reader long enough to impart your wisdom or fact. Consider how you want the reader to feel when reading your book, which may influence how well they take the information in.

In Summary

- **Voice and tone in nonfiction:** Voice and tone are especially important in nonfiction for engaging readers, particularly if your subject could be dry or dense with facts.

- **Personalize the factual:** Adding personal stories or experiences is always a relatable way to make complex subjects more accessible.

- **Humor and playfulness:** If it feels right, even some serious topics can benefit from a lighter, more humorous tone to make it easier for readers to connect to the information.

- **Objective vs. subjective:** Achieving true objectivity in nonfiction is challenging, as biases inevitably shape our experiences. Strive for balance, but don't lean into "false balance" either. When possible, acknowledge your personal experiences.

- **Voice in instructional nonfiction:** Even instructional books can benefit from an engaging voice that blends clear, helpful advice with personality to make learning more enjoyable.

- **Weaving in other stories:** Utilize other mythology or stories to enhance your message or serve as an analogy for your points.

VOICE LESSONS

Writing Exercises

Now, you give it a try!

Personal Story Integration

Choose a factual or instructional topic to write about and introduce it or "interrupt it" with a short personal story or vignette that relates to it. This can help you balance objectivity with a more relatable, personal voice.

Humor in Nonfiction

Take a serious or technical paragraph from something you're working on and rewrite it with a playful or humorous tone. See if you can still convey the core message while making it more engaging and fun.

Bias Check

Identify a topic you're writing about where you have strong opinions. Write a short paragraph acknowledging your perspective and biases, then rewrite it with the goal of removing those biases, ensuring your tone becomes more neutral and objective.

VOICE IN NONFICTION. BALANCING OBJECTIVITY AND PERSONALITY

> "*Invention, it may be humbly admitted, does not consist in creating out of void, but out of chaos.*"
>
> —Mary Shelley

CHAPTER 17

Experimenting with Voice

Experiments in Voice

One of the best parts about being a writer is that you aren't limited to only one voice or one form. If you're writing fiction, you often have the opportunity to write from the perspective of several different character voices. In memoir, you are often "capturing" the voice of other people in your own story in addition to your own, embodying them to best of your experience or recollection. And if you find that a straightforward narrative or one manner of voice isn't enough or isn't working for your story, you also have room to experiment, play, push yourself outside of expected voice constraints.

To illustrate this, we'll wander through a few different techniques in the work of many skilled writers that reveal a multitude of ways to weave in voice, to play with form, and to write unique truths.

Voice Devices

Voice can be expressed through a multitude of forms and literary devices, ranging from letters to diary entries, to stories-within-stories to hermit crab essays (using a borrowed "form" to tell a story, such as a grocery list or a how-to manual), and many more.

To get started looking at some of these, we'll explore Samantha Irby's book of essays *We Are Never Meeting in Real Life*. Many of the essays seem to have their own voice, as though Irby is letting different facets of her personality shine through.

In a hermit crab essay titled, "My Bachelorette Application", she uses the constraints of this application to tell the reader about herself. It launches with a paragraph describing her situation, and then we get into the questions:

> I am squeezed into my push-up bra and sparkly, ill-fitting dress. I've got the requisite sixteen coats of waterproof mascara, black eyeliner, and salmon-colored streaks of hastily applied self tanner drying down the side of my neck. I'm sucking in my stomach, I've taken thirty-seven Imodium in case my irritable bowels have an adverse reaction to the bag of tacos I hid in my purse and ate in the bathroom while no one was looking, and I have been listening to Katy Perry really, really loudly in the limo on the way over here. I'm about to crush a beer can on my forehead. LET'S DO THIS BRO.

EXPERIMENTING WITH VOICE

A few of her answers on the application include these:

Age: 35ish (but I could pass for forty-seven to fifty-two, easily; sixtysomething if I stay up all night)

Gender: Passably female

Weight: Lane Bryant model? But maybe on her period week. I have significantly large ankles.

Occupation: My technical job title is client services director at the animal hospital where I've worked since early 2002, which loosely translates to "surly phone answerer and unfriendly door opener." I'm pretty lazy, although I *am* quite good at playing the race card and eating other people's lunches in the break room.

Do you have any children? I'm counting the cat here. So, yes.

The tone of most of Irby's essays is humorous and self-deprecating, and she rarely takes herself too seriously, though there are notes of seriousness woven throughout. This one has a madcap vibe, as though ripped from a "Three Stooges" routine if they were all women. This voice is sardonic and silly, utilizing some great juxtaposition of what feels like a quintessential, even stereotypical, "feminine" moment of being obsessed with how she looks, then contrasting with the frat-boy energy of crushing a beer can on her head.

Now check out the voice of another of Irby's essays in the same book titled "Mavis", told in a more straightforward form—about the woman she would go on to marry:

> I had ripped the tender flesh on my finger trying to open a piece of mail that wasn't even fucking mine, a fancy wedding invitation on creamy heavyweight card stock intended for some girl named Alicia who lived downstairs in apartment 209. Blood splattered across the velvety envelope while I raced frantically around my kitchen, sucking my finger and snatching open drawers in search of your grandma's favorite adhesive bandages, the thick stretchy fabric kind that conform to every wrinkly crevice.

Here, the tone is not quite as hilariously slapstick, though her signature devil-may-care humor is still intact, with her preferred use of run-on sentences and lots of details, many things happening at once.

Experiments in Form

Now onto a completely different style of book. Jenny Offill's *Dept. of Speculation* is ostensibly a novel about a couple whose marriage is unraveling, but it reads more like a road map back to the source of that rupture as the narrator retraces the events that have led to their breakup. The whole book is written in fragments, as though taking inventory of the relationship. Each paragraph below appears as it does in the book, without indentations and white space between each paragraph. I've chosen a few at random. They tell a story, but not in a linear or cohesive way. More like a series of images you must put together to make a mosaic.

> Memories are microscopic. Tiny particles that swarm together and apart. Little people, Edison called them. Entities. He had a theory about where they came from and that theory was outer space.

> My plan was to never get married. I was going to be an art monster instead. Women almost never become art monsters because art monsters only concern themselves with art, never mundane things. Nabokov didn't even fold his own umbrella. Vera licked his stamps for him.

> Hard to believe I used to think love was such a fragile business. Once when he was still young, I saw a bit of his scalp showing through his hair and I was afraid. But it was just a cowlick. Now sometimes it shows through for real, but I feel only tenderness.

For some people, the floating, disparate nature of the fragments might make it hard to cohere to a voice, but I like the way it feels like you're getting only the essentials, the key snapshots, that make up their life together and their unraveling. I found it to be a cool way to experience a character and a story.

Another interesting device is to invoke multiple voices is utilizing the "story within a story" technique. This might look like one character telling another's story, reading someone's account or diary, or some other variation.

In Leni Zumas's novel *Red Clocks* (which I thought was dystopian at the time it was published *in 2018*, because abortion is outlawed, fetuses are granted personhood, and single women are about to lose their right to adopt), one of the protagonists, Ro, a high school teacher, is pursuing motherhood and writing a biography of a little-known nineteenth-century female polar explorer, Eivør Mínervudottír.

In between chapters featuring the POV of each of the four protagonists, who have quite distinctive voices, we get little passages about Eivør.

> The Polar explorer Eivør Mínervudottír spent many hours, as a child, in the sea-washed lighthouse whose keeper was her uncle.
>
> She knew not to talk while he was making entries in the record book.
>
> Never to strike a match unsupervised.
>
> Red sky at night, sailor's delight.
>
> To keep her head low in the lantern room.
>
> To pee in the pot and leave it, and if she did caca, to wrap it in fish paper for the garbage box.

I love the story within the story because although readers are not directly in Eivør's POV, her voice rises from the tomb of history and "speaks" to the women in the front story, all of whom are grappling with losing their rights, and potentially their voices. Her story suggests to the women of the future (and thus the reader) that they should not give up hope, that they matter, that women always find a way.

Another variation of this story-within-a-story theme comes from a wonderfully quirky novel called *A Tale for the Time Being,* by Ruth Ozeki. In the aftermath of Japan's devastating 2011 tsunami, debris makes its way all the way across to the Pacific Northwest of the US. Protagonist Ruth (yes, author and protagonist share the same name, and yes, that's on purpose; hello, auto-fiction) finds a diary inside a Hello Kitty lunchbox written by a sixteen-year-old girl named Nao Yasutani. In between chapters of reading Nao's diary, Ozeki alternates chapters of Ruth reading the diary. The book alternates between Ruth's and Nao's POVs.

Here's a piece of the first excerpt of the diary:

> Hi!
>
> My name is Nao, and I am a time being. Do you know what a time being is? Well, if you give me a moment, I will tell you.
>
> A time being is someone who lives in time, and that means you, and me, and every one of us who is, or was, or ever will be. As for me, right now I am sitting in a French maid café in Akiba Electricity Town, listening to a sad chanson that is playing sometime in your past, which is also my present, writing this and wondering about you, somewhere in my future. And

if you're reading this, then maybe by now you're wondering about me, too.

And here's a section from Ruth's POV:

She picked up the diary and, using the side of her thumb, started riffling through the pages. She wasn't reading, in fact she was trying not to…How many diaries and journals had she herself started and then abandoned? How many aborted novels languished in folders on her hard drive? But to her surprise, although the color of the ink occasionally bled from purple to pink to black to blue and back to purple again, the writing itself never faltered, growing smaller and if anything even denser, straight to the very last, tightly packed page. The girl had run out of paper before she ran out of words.

And then?

Ruth snapped the book shut and closed her eyes for good measure to keep herself from cheating and reading the final sentence, but the question lingered, floating like a retinal burn in the darkness of her mind: *What happens in the end?*

These devices allow the reader access to multiple voices, and for those voices to inform and affect the characters as well.

Second Person

Another charming voice convention is when the writer opts for the second person. I find it particularly delightful when it is done in essay or memoir, where we are expecting the "I" POV but instead get that deeply interior second-person "you" instead.

Here's an example from the titular essay titled "How to Skin a Bird" in Chelsea Biondolillo's book of essays, *The Skinned Bird*.

> Your first and only incision will be right over the sternum. All birds have a bald patch there. Blow lightly on the breast until the feathers begin to part and you can see the pale skin beneath.
>
> Rest your finger there for a moment. Feel the bone your blade will follow. Make a wish, if you must, and then slice from collar to belly carefully.

These second-person passages could be read as the narrator reading following instructions on this difficult, morbid, but necessary act, or they could be read as a close internal dialogue the narrator is having with herself. There's a subtle tone of menace and melancholy in the second-person passages. Notice how different the next paragraph reads, where she reverts to first person.

> I used to keep the letters my father had written to me in a box with all of my other letters. There were three of them, all written before I was eight, on lined paper

with a ripped, spiral fringe.

The essay alternates between these voices, offering an intimacy through the act of skinning the bird. It begins to feel as though the narrator is skinning *herself*, peeling away what is protective to reveal the painful truth of her relationship with her father.

In another example, one of my favorite authors and people, Gayle Brandeis, drops into the third person to simulate disassociation in one passage of her memoir, *The Art of Misdiagnosis: Surviving My Mother's Suicide.* The memoir takes place after her mother's unexpected suicide and weaves Gayle's own narrative, letters she writes posthumously to her mother, transcripts of her mother's documentary on illness, and research on delusional and factitious disorders.

Here is the passage that takes place just after Gayle has learned of her mother's shocking death, which also comes not long after she's given birth to her third child.

> The older daughter splits in half. She hears weird guttural sounds coming out of her throat, but she doesn't feel them. Half of her has left her body, observes herself in grief. She turns to her husband, Michael—he is making strange sounds, too, his mouth twisted into a Mobius strip—it doesn't look real, his mouth, his pain.

The third person so beautifully captures disassociation, the way one's mind can separate from the body in the face of traumatic or shocking news.

It's notably different from when she writes to her mother (after death, each passage steeped in grief).

> Dear Mom,
>
> My therapist suggested I write to you. She thought it might help me find some clarity, help me understand how I am feeling about everything. It's good advice—I often don't know what I know until I write it down.
>
> I wish I knew where to begin.
>
> I supposed I could just write
>
> WHY?
>
> In giant letters smack in the middle of the page and leave it at that. I could be more specific: "Why did you kill yourself?" But even that would be too easy. Besides, I have too many other questions. Questions about our family's relationship with illness. Questions about our family's relationship with silence. Questions about your own relationship with your family. Questions, questions, so very many questions. Questions you'll never be able to answer.
>
> It's always been hard to talk to you.

Lastly, Brandeis intersperses transcripts from her mother's documentary that explored Arlene's childhood bout of rheumatic fever, Gayle's childhood grappling with Crohn's disease, and her sister's eating disorder (some of which will turn out to have been fabricated by her mother).

One more "experiment" comes from the stunning short-story collection *The Secret Lives of Church Ladies* by Deesha Philyaw. In the short story "How to Make Love to a Physicist" the title refrain (hark back to our lesson on anaphora) carries us through different pieces of the story, acting like connective tissue or dark matter that holds the cosmos of the story together. Also written in the second person, Philyaw tells a love story that interweaves science and race and faith and desire. (The ellipses are mine, showing that I've excerpted sections.)

> **How do you make love to a physicist?** You do it on Pi Day—pi is a constant, also irrational—but the groundwork is laid months in advance.
>
> ...
>
> **How do you make love to a physicist?** On the flight home from the conference, you tally all the things you have in common:
>
> You're tired of people asking why you're still single
>
> You care about children, but don't want any of your own
>
> Fall is your favorite season
>
> You're not a fan of Tyler Perry, and you're tired of people insisting you become one...
>
> ...
>
> **How do you make love to a physicist?** Ask him if he believes in God. Ask him if he thinks it's possible to reconcile science and religion.

I love how the use of the refrain "How do you make love to a physicist" cuts away from the need to fill in explanatory details between sections. It allows her to control the narrative and shape the voice.

In truth, calling any of these "experiments" is a little silly; literature is comprised of numerous styles, forms, and voices. These narratives may depart from a straightforward narrative arc you were taught in school, or they may play with voice in less than linear ways, but they are all still relatable ways to connect with the reader. Hopefully, they empower you to find the right forms for the projects you're working on, and allow you to not feel limited by some canon or mindset you learned in school but that may not feel true to your story.

In Summary

- **Voice flexibility:** Don't feel married to one voice if you find experimenting with multiple voices, perspectives, and / or forms within a single piece feels truer to the story you're trying to tell.

- **Experiment with form:** Don't feel limited by one form. Draw from many forms (like the hermit crab essay, fragmented narratives, second-person narration, and stories-within-stories) to bring unique layers to your story.

- **Story-within-a-story technique:** Play with finding a story within the story, incorporating another voice whose story can be told within / alongside the primary one.

- **Second-person narration:** Depart from first-person POV through the second person to allow for a heightened intimacy with the narrator or character voice.

- **Third person as emotional detachment:** Try utilizing third person and other techniques to show emotional dissociation during traumatic experiences.

VOICE LESSONS

Writing Exercises

Now, you give it a try!

Hermit Crab Essay

Choose a nonliterary form—such as a grocery list, recipe, job application, or instructional manual—and use it to tell a short personal story—whether based in truth (memoir / essay) or a fictionalized variation. Let the voice of your character or narrator stay authentic despite the constraints of the form.

Second-Person Experiment

Rewrite a short personal memory of your narrator or character that was previously in first person POV into second person, as if you're narrating the memory back to yourself. What changes in the story as a result? Does it feel more or less "true" for the character or narrator?

Story Within a Story

Write a brief scene in which one character recounts a separate short story or anecdote to another character. Pay attention to how the storytelling character's voice differs from their normal dialogue, and how the embedded story reveals something new or surprising about them.

> "They knew their voices broke a silence of a thousand million years, the silence of wind and leaves and wind, blowing and ceasing and blowing again."
>
> —URSULA K. LE GUIN, *THE ONES WHO WALK AWAY FROM OMELAS*

CHAPTER 18

The Power and Evolution of Voice

The Power of Voice

For this final chapter, I want to talk to you directly about *your own voice* before we finish by talking about how voices evolve and change.

Anyone who has ever felt voiceless knows the delicate balance of the power of being heard and the agony of being restricted from using yours. You can't speak about voice—in the larger sense of freedom to express or communicate—without talking about power, who has it and who wants it, who uses it to oppress, and who shares it. Just look at how indigenous children were taken from their tribal nations and deprived of their language and culture in boarding schools. Voice is power. Voice is freedom. Look at how women's voices have been pushed aside, suppressed, and only painfully, slowly introduced into just about every great field of study for centuries. Voice is authority. Voice is creation.

As the #ownvoices movement gained steam in the last few years, it has sought to encourage publishers to produce more books in which historically silenced people tell their own stories, be they Indigenous Americans and other people of color, women, queer folks, or those with disabilities and neurodivergencies, to name a few. Anyone who has struggled to find representation of themselves in books or film will tell you how much it matters to feel heard, how finding voices like yours can not only be life affirming, but *lifesaving*. How many of us turned to books as children (and still do as adults) to survive difficult times, even trauma? I know I did.

If you live in the US, then voice is also protected by the constitution in the First Amendment, the freedom of speech. No matter where you fall on the political divide, remember how important it is to exercise your right to that freedom and to insist that everyone have that same right. Where would we be without the great journalists and philosophers, the activists and critics who speak truth to power, often when it is unpopular? Where would we be without bell hooks, Gloria Steinem, Marsha P. Johnson, Grace Lee Boggs, or Malala Yousafzai?

Whenever you can, be that voice.

This is all to say that your voice matters. Supremely.

Whether to one other individual, or to a collective. The unique perspectives, attitudes, opinions, and observations you have earned by living on this planet are valuable, whether they flow out in fictional characters enacting cool plots or come forth as a personal memoir about a specific time in your life.

It's equally important to recognize if your voice is running over someone who deserves to be heard—whether that's trying to tell a story that really isn't yours to tell or not making room for a plenitude of other voices. Try to make room for and bring other voices along with yours whenever you can.

Voices Change

Let's talk about change, that inevitability in everything, including writing and voice. If you've kept any kind of diary, journal, or account of your life and chanced a look backward some years, I'm sure you know that squirmy experience of looking at a past version of yourself, at an outdated-seeming voice, and feeling a little embarrassed, surprised, or amused. As you change, so often does your voice and your *perception* of your voice. I can't even read Facebook status updates from more than a few years ago without cringing, much less the journals I kept as a teenager and as a twentysomething. Frankly, if you only read my teen journals, I'd forgive you for thinking I didn't have an intelligent thought in my head past pursuing my latest crush.

Don't be afraid of your written voice changing. It's not only inevitable, but it can be wonderful to chart your own evolution (and very useful to the memoir / essay writer). Since voice is comprised of the complex web of personal elements we've discussed so far, then there's simply no way your written voice *could* stay the same.

I thought it would be fun to look at a couple of authors who have been writing for decades, to see how their written voices have changed. Now, this isn't a straight line because some of these books may not even be in the same genre, and we're not doing this exercise to judge the writing at either stage as "bad" or "good," only different. But it's still interesting.

I'll start with one of my all-time favorite authors, novelist Louise Erdrich, whose more than twenty-eight novels often address the complexities of her heritage as a member of the Ojibwe tribe. I first read her novel *Love Medicine* as a teenager in the 1980s (it was published in 1984) and was hooked. Here's a passage from her novel *The Bingo Palace*, about an indigenous character named Lipsha Morrissey who is summoned by his grandmother to the reservation, where he must come to terms with his heritage and his future path.

> On most winter days, Lulu Lamartine did not stir until the sun cast a patch of warmth for her to bask in and purr. She then rose, brewed fresh coffee, heated a pan of cream, and drank the mix from a china cup at

THE POWER AND EVOLUTION OF VOICE

her apartment table. Sipping, brooding, she entered the snowy world. A pale sweet roll, a doughnut gem, occasionally a bowl of cereal, followed that coffee, then more coffee, and on and on, until finally Lulu pronounced herself awake and took on the day's business of running the tribe.

Here's a novel of hers published in 2017, titled *Future Home of the Living God*, in which evolution appears to be stopping its forward momentum and pregnant people are being hunted down, caught, and studied.

> When I tell you that my white name is Cedar Hawk Songmaker and that I am the adopted child of Minneapolis liberals, and that when I went looking for my Ojibwe parents and found that I was born Mary Potts I hid that knowledge, maybe you'll understand. Or not. I'll write this anyway, because ever since last week things have changed. Apparently—I mean, nobody knows—our world is running backward.

The difference in voices is notable to me in that the first is very lyrical and dreamy, taking its time getting to anything like plot. If you read any of Erdrich's early books, that lyrical voice is often present—as much the ghost of the author in every sentence as it is the characters speaking for themselves. The voice in the second novel, published twenty-three years after the first, is more concrete and direct, and feels planted firmly inside the character's head.

Let's do it again with another of my favorite authors, Barbara Kingsolver. In her novel *The Bean Trees*, published in 1988, protagonist Taylor Green is fleeing her rural Kentucky town before she winds up pregnant and without prospects. Yet she ends up in Arizona as the unofficial guardian of a three-year-old American Indian child named Turtle.

> I have been afraid of putting air in a tire ever since I saw a tractor tire blow up and throw Newt Hardbine's father over the top of the Standard Oil sign. I'm not lying. He got stuck up there. About nineteen people congregated during the time it took for Norman Strick to walk up to the Courthouse and blow the whistle for the volunteer fire department.

And we'll contrast it with her Pulitzer Prize-winning novel *Demon Copperhead*, a novel set in southern Appalachia, in which protagonist Demon is described as "with no assets beyond his dead father's good looks and copper-colored hair, a caustic wit, and a fierce talent for survival…braves the modern perils of foster care, child labor, derelict schools, athletic success, addiction, disastrous loves, and crushing losses," according to the book jacket. It was published in 2022, some thirty-four years later.

> First, I got myself born. A decent crowd was on hand to watch, and they've always given me that much: the worst of the job was up to me, my mother being let's just say out of it.
>
> On any other day they'd have seen her outside on the deck of her trailer home, good neighbors taking notice,

pestering the tit of trouble as they will. All through the dog-breath air of late summer and fall, cast an eye up the mountain and there she'd be, little bleach-blonde smoking her Pall Malls, hanging on that railing like she's captain of her ship up there and now might be the hour it's going down. This is an eighteen-year-old girl we're discussing, all on her own and as pregnant as it gets.

If Erdrich's work in the two examples got a little less voice-heavy and lyrical over time, Kingsolver's grew voice-heavier, richer, full of music and movement.

When Voices Must Stay the Same

For every voice that changes over time, there are some that must stay relatively the same, particularly in a series in which the stories are driven by a voicey character that keeps bringing readers back.

From Janet Evanovich's sharp-cracking and witty bounty hunter Stephanie Plum in her mystery novels; to Diana Gabaldon's resourceful, headstrong, and independent time-traveling healer; to Claire Fraser in the *Outlander* series; to the philosophical dry wit of Easy Rawlins, the detective in Walter Mosley's noir mysteries; while these characters do change, they also stay the "same." In these instances, there are personality quirks and characteristics the reader comes to expect, and which the authors deliver.

In other kinds of nonfiction, as discussed in Chapter

16, the voice is likely to remain much the same throughout the entire book unless you're purposely playing with different voices throughout it.

Adapting Voice for Different Audiences

Some of you may have a chosen form or genre that you stay true to, while others of you may find you prefer to write across multiple forms or voices. If the latter is true, and you're new to shifting genre or form, it can feel a little overwhelming at first. It's not uncommon for me to edit a first novel written by someone who has not considered themselves a fiction writer—for instance, people from a wide variety of careers, from military backgrounds to accounting, who must learn to create or find a new voice. It's also not uncommon for someone with a history of journalism skills or technical writing to try their hand at something more creative.

This is where thinking of your audience can be helpful. If you're trying to adopt a voice you're comfortable with into one that's new, here are some tips that might help:

- **Consider your audience.** While thinking about your reader the entire time you write may not be helpful, it might be useful if you're making a shift between voices or forms. When I write an article, for example, I know my audience is seeking education and information. When I write a novel, I imagine my audience wants to be entertained and engaged with the characters in my story. I certainly don't write those two forms in the same way or with the same voice.

- **Create a persona.** If possible, imagine each version of you writing in a particular voice as a different self, a persona. It's why it's so important to remind memoirists and essayists that they are as much curators of their own experiences as they are the ones who lived it, because so much of writing is about *shaping* experience. If you presented most experiences exactly as they happened, beat by beat, it would likely be full of boring filler. You can even come up with different attributes for each voice / form—how "they" look and sound, their background, their experiences, and so on.

- **Syntax and word choice.** Reflecting back on the discussion of syntax and lexicon, by intentionally choosing different kinds of sentence structure, vocabulary, and concrete nouns, adjectives, and verbs in one voice over another, you can start to distinguish these voices from one another.

THE SOUND OF STORY

Voice in the Age of AI

I also want to say a few words about voice in the age of artificial intelligence (AI), though I don't want to linger here. On the one hand, technology in and of itself is neither harmful nor good; the danger lies the way that technology is used. That may also be true of AI as it's being used in writing, largely through large language models like ChatGPT and DeepSeek (and no, I'm not in love with AI as a tool of creative writing, maybe because I grew up in the age of dinosaurs before everyone had so much as a personal computer, much less a handheld supercomputer phone). All that said, AI is likely here to stay. If you're using AI to draft something, or even write it outright, consider several important factors: AI is only as good as its training inputs (which are human), and just like when you pour many colors of paint into one bucket and get "mud," AI often reduces the wonderful unique things about voice down to a less unique signature. Yes, you can ask it to write you a poem in the style of e. e. cummings, or to write you a term paper, but remember, that leaves out one essential piece: *you*. Your voice, your creativity, your passion.

 That said, if you need to write something serviceable—a contract, a press release, etc., AI can be great for drafting basic information. Just be sure, whenever possible, to flesh it out with your own voice.

 Moreover, remember that while AI is a great mimic,

it has borrowed from its inputs, which are human-created. ChatGPT is controversial in that it was essentially trained on the entire internet up until about 2019, including books and articles without those authors' permission. Meta's LibGen was trained on millions of authors' work without permission. So, while it may sound clever or smart, in truth, AI is nothing more than a highly sophisticated mimic. What AI can't do is bring human empathy, heart, and feeling to the work. Only you can do that.

Before You Go

At the end of this book, I hope you take away the deep connection between character / narrator and voice—that the "sound" of a character is soaked in our experiences as well as the sentence-level tricks that make language so lush. If you're writing about your own life, you already have all the ingredients for voice wrapped up inside you; you may just need permission to let it loose. At the end of the day, I believe everyone, fictional or real, wants to be heard in one form or another—and now, I hope you have a few more tools to do so.

Online Sources Referenced

1. "Passive voice." Hamilton University. https://www.hamilton.edu/academics/centers/writing/seven-sins-of-writing/1

2. Sidnell, Jack. "African American Vernacular English." University of Hawaii. https://www.hawaii.edu/satocenter/langnet/definitions/aave.html

3. "Null Copula." Yale Grammatical Diversity Project. English in North America. Yale University. https://ygdp.yale.edu/phenomena/null-copula

4. Bey, Marquis. "Jargon for the Blacks—and Others." *Black Perspectives*—African American Intellectual History Society. September 30, 2019. https://www.aaihs.org/jargon-for-the-blacks-and-others/

5. Darwin, Emma. "Plain and Perfect, Rich and Rare: What Is 'Lyrical' Writing?" This Itch of Writing blog. May 20, 2013 https://emma-darwin.typepad.com/thisitchofwriting/2013/05/plain-and-perfect-rich-and-rare.html

6. Munger, D. "Alliteration improves memory performance." ScienceBlogs. August 29, 2008. https://scienceblogs.com/cognitivedaily/2008/08/29/alliteration-improves-memory-p#google_vignette

7. Lynch, Maura M. "A Conversation with Sally Rooney." *Stet Magazine*. April 23, 2018. https://stetmag.com/interviews/sally-rooney-interview-conversations-with-friends

8. Grimes, David Robert. "Impartial journalism is laudable. But false balance is dangerous." *The Guardian*. November 8, 2016. https://www.theguardian.com/science/blog/2016/nov/08/impartial-journalism-is-laudable-but-false-balance-is-dangerous

Learn More about Sibyl Writing Craft Books and Courses

PHOTO CREDIT: Tara Sturtevant

About the Author

Jordan Rosenfeld is a writer, mentor, avid reader and word nerd having spent over 25 years elbow-deep in story craft, exploring what makes characters leap off the page, and keeps readers turning them. With seven books on writing craft and three novels of her own, she doesn't just talk about writing—she lives it, wrestles with it, and helps you understand its mess and magic. Whether you're wrangling a first draft or polishing for publication, Jordan works closely with fiction and memoir writers to sharpen their skills from the sentence level to the story arc.

Acknowledgments

This book could not have been written without the examples of numerous books by authors across many genres. Can I literally thank every author I have ever read, because their words have forged me?! I am also lucky to be someone who gets to read widely for work, but I also recommend doing so to improve your own voice and tone. Sometimes we hone ours by recognizing what it is *not*.

To my husband Erik and my son Ben, who make everything worth doing.

This book has been percolating in my brain for years as I've taught a series of workshops on the same concepts but wasn't entirely sure if it could be adapted into a book. Thanks to the incredible Sibylline Press team, it turns out it very much could: Vicki DeArmon, Julia Park Tracey, Suzy Vitello, Anna Termine, Hannah Rutkowski, and Sang Kim. Plus Alicia Feltman for her gorgeous (as always) cover and Jennifer Safrey for copyediting.

Thanks to Craig Lore for a careful read that helped me refresh grammar terms I'd blocked out since eighth-grade English; Dayna Bennett for helping further with clarity and flow; Stacey Parshall Brown for her sensitivity reading; and all the English professors I've ever had, who may not have made me love grammar but never made me hate writing.

Gratitude also goes to the people who supported my writing life during the writing of this book through listening ears, kvetching, crying, camaraderie, and understanding: Dayna Bennett, Kerra Bolton, Laura Bogart, Cindy Lamothe, and Levi Leidy have been great friends and support. Thanks to the "friends of JR book club" who talk literature with me so delightfully each month, especially founding members Whitney Pintello, Katie Khera, and Craig Lore. I'm also grateful to my friend and author Steven Dunn, whose workshop "Writing Sentences That Feel" and a referral to the work of Reuven Tsur have been great guides in my writing and teaching.

I also don't think I'd have made it through a pandemic and political upheaval, not to mention my creative life, without my writing students who have stuck with me through the years and given me purpose and community, even in the darkest of times, especially: Rita, Susan, Moe, Michelle, Sean, Vance, Cat, Jack, Wendy, Erin, Marty, Dawn, and, of course, Bob, to name a few.

Finally, to my nephew Odin and niece Marlowe, who have no trouble proudly using their voices—may that always remain the same.

How to Write Stunning Sentences • Living the Life: Writing Vivid, Memorable Characters • The Joys and Challenges of Revision: A Hands-on Approach to Forming and Finishing a Project for Publication • A Writer's Resolution: Setting Your Goals for the New Year • The Sound of Story—Finding, Crafting and Playing with Voice • 'Tude and Tone: How Attitude and Opinion Shape Page Turning Characters • Voice and POV: Shifting Perspectives, Shifting Voice • When the Character is You: Curating Voice in the Memoir or Essay • Voice Up Your Non-Fiction: How to Capture and Keep Reader Attention • Tone, Emotion and Mood: Controlling Your Readers' Feelings • The Sound of Story—Finding Crafting and Playing with Voice • Lyrical Writing For Plot-Forward Writers • Revising for Voice: Polishing This Key Element of Successful Writing • Experiments in Voice: Breaking Free From Usual Forms • Sound of Story: Voice and Tone Immersion • Looking to the Past: How to Research your Historical Fiction • Writing from Multiple Viewpoints • The Tough Love Publishing Intensive: Get Real. Get Ready. Get Published • Path to Publication • Are You Actually Ready to Publish? • Ask Us Anything — Live Publishing Strategy Q&A • One Book Won't Pay the Bills: Real Talk About Author Income, Career Growth, and Making It Work • Social Media for Authors: The Good, the Bad, and the Absolutely Necessary • Pitch Perfect: Sell Your Book to Bookstores, Libraries, and Gatekeepers • Understanding Rights and Licensing • Understanding the World of Book Publishing • Acquisitions for Noobs: How to get through the door! • On the Frontlines with Bookstores • Bookstore Presentation Coaching by an Expert

Learn more about our books and courses!

SIBYL WRITING CRAFT

Books and Courses Designed for Writers

Sibylline Press is thrilled to introduce our new writing craft series paired with online writing courses.

Sibyl Writing Craft's 2026 courses include 30 different offerings taught by our instructors, each dedicated to different aspects of writing and the business of book publishing. Our instructors (we call them mentors) are women of a certain age with years of wisdom and experience and they include many of our partners at Sibylline Press. And yes, we are all writers as well.

Each year, as writers, we think about what we will accomplish in the coming year. We set our goals and revisit our ambitions. It may be to improve some aspect of our craft, to hone the work we have, to start something new, to achieve publication, or to jumpstart our author skills once published.

At Sibyl Writing Craft, we can revel with you at the sentence level or help you polish your manuscripts using the tools of voice, tone, character, and point of view, to name a few. We can assist with your revisions. We can walk you through the book industry and how it really works. We can shed light on how licensing and rights work or train you on social media. We can provide a road map for indie authors to capitalize on every opportunity. We can train you to present to bookstores. We know you will delight in our range offerings as much as we delighted in creating them.

Our courses are designed as Confabs, which are 75-minute informational talks on a topic, and the longer Labs, which provide more interactivity for participants on a given subject over three or more sessions. Each Confab or Lab comes with one of our Sibyl Writing Craft books on that subject and is taught by that author. Most Confabs and Labs take place on Zoom. Some take place in partner bookstores.

In addition to offering fabulous courses, we've got gifts. Upon enrollment in our Confabs or Labs this first year, you'll receive a complimentary copy of *A Writer's Resolution*. This writer's journal will help you plan your writing future.

We can't wait to collaborate with you on your writing and publishing journey. We are invested in your success as a writer. And as a book publisher, the team at Sibylline Press even hopes to see your best work in our submissions portal.

 To learn more about our Confabs or Labs for the year, please see our catalog at sibyllinepress.com.

SIBYL WRITING CRAFT

Titles Coming in 2026

PLUS: *A Writer's Resolution: A Guided Journal for Realizing a Rewarding Writing Practice* By Christine Walker

www.ingramcontent.com/pod-product-compliance
Lightning Source LLC
Chambersburg PA
CBHW031425160426
43195CB00010BB/620